# OTHER WORLDS

THE ENDLESS
POSSIBILITIES
OF
LITERATURE

D1417752

# OTHER WORLDS

## THE ENDLESS POSSIBILITIES OF LITERATURE

Trevor H. Cairney

Heinemann
Portsmouth, New Hampshire

**Heinemann Educational Books, Inc.**
361 Hanover Street, Portsmouth, NH 03801-3959
Offices and agents throughout the world.

Copyright © 1990 and 1991 by Trevor Cairney

First U.S. edition published 1991.

Library of Congress Cataloging-in-Publication Data

Cairney, Trevor.
    Other worlds: the endless possibilities of literature / by Trevor
H. Cairney. — 1st U.S. ed.
        p. cm.
Includes bibliographical references (p.     ).
ISBN 0–435–08531–X
1. Reading (Elementary) 2. Literature–Study and teaching
(Elementary) 3. Children–Books and reading. I. Title.
LB1573.C166 1990
372.4–dc20                                                    90-30709
                                                                    CIP

All rights reserved. No part of this publication may be reproduced
in any form of electronic or mechanical means, including
information storage and retrieval systems, without permission in
writing from the publisher, Heinemann Educational Books, Inc.,
361 Hanover Street, Portsmouth, NH 03801, USA except by
a reviewer, who may quote brief passages in a review.

Designed by Richard Tabaka
Cover design by Diana Murray
Computer page composition by ID Studio, Sydney

# Contents

# Foreword

The aim of this book is to help teachers create communities of readers and writers. It is based upon two major premises. First, classrooms should be places that provide opportunities for students to learn about language as they relate to other people. Reading is inherently social, and as such is learned as an extension of the relationships that exist with other people. Second, books are vehicles that can transport readers into other worlds. They are not vessels containing meaning which is waiting to be consumed. Rather they are written blueprints which readers use to construct meaning. In essence, they are doorways to other worlds, providing endless possibilities for the making of meaning.

In the early chapters of this book these premises are expanded, and the roles of the teacher and the child explored. Chapters 1 to 6 explain how and why teachers should create communities of readers and writers, and describe in detail the type of literary environment which I believe is important. The latter chapters attempt to show how the endless possibilities of literature can be explored in classrooms. In providing detailed literature programs the aim has not been to provide short cuts to literacy — none exist! Rather, my aim has been to give the reader an insight into the type of programs I use within classrooms.

In outlining detailed programs in a book like this, there is the danger the reader will be left with the impression that the place reading assumes in my classrooms is always a well-ordered one, that literature is one of a number of components that I managed to slot into a busy program. However, this could not be further from the truth. The literary environment that I hope you will create after reading this book is one where the unexpected is given opportunity to emerge, where readers spontaneously share their excitement and discoveries about books with those who they know have also discovered the pleasure, joy and excitement of literature.

In writing this book I owe a great deal to the many children who I have taught. The insights gained from talking to children about literature have had a profound effect upon the way I teach. I never cease to be amazed by the discoveries children make as they 'live through' books. Their discoveries have stretched me as a reader, teacher and person. As well, I am indebted to many colleagues who have had an impact upon me as a teacher. Mrs Boscato (the school librarian in my first year of teaching); Don Holdaway whose book *Independence in Reading* (1972; second edition, 1980) transformed my teaching; Jerry Harste who challenged *all* my assumptions about language and learning when I spent six months with him in 1984; members of the Riverina Literacy Team with whom I worked for three and a half years, and Rhonda Jenkins and Beverley Weynton who read and responded to the manuscript of this book.

Finally, I am indebted to my own special literary community — my wife Carmen and my two book-devouring daughters Nicole and Louise. Our joint love of literature has probably been the single most important factor in my growth as a teacher of reading; we have explored the endless possibilities of literature together. My hope is that this book will help teachers to create classroom environments in which students make these discoveries for themselves.

# CHAPTER ONE

# Building Communities of Readers and Writers

In *The Stone Book Quartet* (Garner 1988), a small Welsh girl, Mary, is led by her father towards an understanding of secret truths known only to specific members of her family across the generations. Mary longs for a book so she can learn to read and be like other more 'privileged' children in the village. But her father mistrusts the books of the learned, and chooses instead to use the objects of the earth to 'read' the history of the world. He suggests that many stories can be found in the rocks he quarries and fashions into buildings. When Mary asks for a book he gives her one fashioned from stone, and tells her that unlike an ordinary book which has 'only one story' (p. 58), this book contains 'all the stories of the world' (p. 61).

Garner's old Welsh stonemason is the perfect place to start this book about literature. In him we are confronted by two important themes that will shape the character of this book. First, Mary's father provides a perfect starting point to challenge the age-old assumption that a book has 'only one story'. An assumption, I should add, which has placed great limits on the sharing and study of literature. I will argue that books, like the earth that the old man values so highly, offer endless possibilities for creating meaning — access to 'all the stories of the world'. Second, her father leads Mary to discover the potential that the earth has to inform and shape us. In relationship to her father, and other people who surround her, Mary learns to unravel the history of the world from the objects of the earth.

In the same way, children learn to read the word and the world (Freire & Macedo 1987) as an extension of the culture, community and relationships of which they are a part. I will argue in this book that as teachers, we must be concerned for the creation of communities of people, who value and share literature because of the 'stone-like' secrets it invites readers to discover.

This book then, is about literature and how it can be shared. Its focus is the building of communities of people who value and share the stories they construct as they read. I see this as vital because far too often I have observed classrooms where literature has had little significance. I believe this need not be the case, that children can learn to value literature if we create environments in which it is given prominence.

## What do Children Learn about Literacy from the Literary Environment You Create in the Classroom?

As I talk with teachers today I constantly hear the lament that children simply do not want to read. Comments like the following abound:

'It's hard to teach them to read when they're not interested.'

'If only their parents read more to them at home.'

'They watch too much television.'

'When we were kids we used to read books every night.'

I find these statements anomalous in a society where books are so prevalent. In the 18th and 19th centuries schools adopted the role of teachers of literacy because most homes were not rich sites of literacy. Only the wealthy had books (and could read them), and for children, most literary experiences came as part of other social activities — for example, church. For most, books were not a part of their world. The irony for us as teachers today is that people have more books in their homes than at any time in the history of the world. And yet, for many children, reading is still not a significant part of their lives.

Our problem in the 1980s and 1990s is quite different to that in the 1780s. Schools have done an effective job teaching children to read in western cultures, but have achieved this by creating a new kind of reading which has legitimacy only within the school. Children can read, but rarely do, for purposes other than those prescribed by school. The major challenge for literacy educators is to redress this problem.

I believe one of the keys is for teachers to reshape the classroom communities of which they are a part.

For many children, reading has become little more than a school subject, with basal readers, worksheets and reading laboratories dominating instruction. The classrooms in which these children learn are characterised by a number of features which effectively reinforce dysfunctional notions about literacy. In these classrooms children:

- rarely choose books to read for purposes they see as legitimate
- are forced to read books and materials unlike reading matter in the 'real world'
- are given few opportunities to share discoveries about literacy
- are not encouraged to share responses to reading with other members of their class
- fail to discover that reading and writing have many useful functions in the real world.

It should not be surprising then, to find children who only ever experience reading as something they do at school, who fail to see that it is an important part of their world. Reading is viewed by many children as an activity to which they must submit, and books, as something containing words to be consumed (Cairney 1985b). For these children, reading is rarely seen as something to be enjoyed and used for learning. Traditional school practices, like the use of basal reading programs, have indirectly taught children that they read so the teacher can either test them, or provide an activity afterwards.

In a recent research project (Cairney 1988a) I interviewed 179 children and asked a variety of questions designed to elicit perceptions of the purpose of specific classroom reading practices. In particular, I looked at student understanding of the purposes for basal readers, the most common source of reading material in Australian classrooms. Predictably, children rarely mentioned enjoyment and a search for meaning as reasons for reading basal readers. More worrying was the perception (which I believe is accurate) by 53% of the students, that the purpose of reading worksheets has little to do with learning to read, a search for meaning and so on. These children saw worksheets as time fillers and devices for permitting teacher testing. One child even commented: 'That's what teachers get paid to do'.

For many children reading has only ever been experienced as a school subject. It has been: given in neatly timetabled timeslots; taught in ability groups; experienced frequently as a boring and frustrating round robin exercise; and based on reading material which has lacked interest and literary quality. Some children reach the end of the first three years of schooling with little more to look back on than basal stories concerning dressing for school, lost hats, and trips to the fire station, airport and zoo (Cairney 1987a). This need not be the case. We need to eradicate the negative demonstrations of literacy that some of our practices provide.

## Building Communities that Value Reading

What we need to do as teachers is create a community of readers and writers, a group of people sharing its discoveries about literacy. Of vital importance to this sense of community are the relationships that arise and are encouraged between its members. Just as Mary in *The Stone Book Quartet* (1988)was introduced to the secrets of the earth in relationship to other people, so too, children learn to read within a complex community of relationships (Cairney 1987a). To illustrate the complexity of these communities and the point I am trying to make, let me share three simple vignettes.

### 1. A kindergarten in the canefields of Queensland

Nineteen small four-year-old faces look up at their teacher as she chats with them about the story *The Three Little Pigs* (Jacobs 1967). The children sit cross-legged on a large carpet square at the front of the room, the venue for news, music, discussion, sharing ideas, and, last but not least, stories. The group has been asked to comment on the story and is responding enthusiastically. Ideas flow quickly as the comment of one child stimulates other responses. The discussion moves from one part of the story to another. Different characters are mentioned, and favourite parts shared. Sometimes the comments relate closely to the story, at other times they are more egocentric. Their attention turns to the big bad wolf and Robert announces 'I've got a big bad wolf and I put him in hot water.' Louise replies, 'My bad wolf got shot with hot rocks.' Christian responds with a somewhat deeper thought 'The wolf got hurt because he tried to hurt the pigs.' The children are part of a small community of language users who delight in the sharing of reading and writing.

These young children attend a kindergarten among the canefields in a coastal town in far North Queensland. The buildings are modest and the fittings and equipment fairly standard. There is a nature table in one corner, large and small building blocks, easels, paints, clay, and a reading corner which is physically appealing. The reading corner includes a brightly covered divan, a few cushions, a variety of books, newspapers and magazines. A sign hangs on the wall asking 'Have You Read Any Good Books Lately?' Artwork displays also show the influence of literature, and group craft efforts depicting characters from books are proudly on show. The teacher in this classroom, Susan Langbien, has been actively attempting to develop a community of readers and writers. As you look around it is plain to see that literacy is an important part of the world of this class.

Each session of the day includes the reading of a piece of poetry or prose. Frequently, these sessions are followed by lively discussion. Daily independent reading time is provided on the carpet area. News time frequently involves the spontaneous sharing of books. Opportunities are provided for response to reading, and this takes many forms — drawing, writing, dramatic re-enactment, mime and singing.

Even when the teacher is not initiating reading or writing, the classroom is filled with literate behaviour. In the dress-up corner several children are including story-reading in creative play. Children take turns as mother reading to her baby. Genevieve is asking her pretend mum to explain why the dog in *I'll Always Love You* (Wilhelm 1985), had such a sad face. Mum does a wonderful job explaining the relationships within the story. Another group playing shops uses a receipt book to record purchases. 'Mum' and 'dad' are reading the newspaper and later flicking through the pages of the telephone book. Everywhere one looks, literate behaviour is to be found (Cairney & Langbien 1989).

## 2. A grade five on the outskirts of Indianapolis

On the first morning in Jean's classroom my presence seemed to cause a buzz. Jean introduced me and said that I was a visitor from Australia and wanted to teach in an American classroom. Endless questions followed: 'Do you have television in Australia?', 'Have you got HBO, (cable television movies) down there?', 'Is there a bridge to Australia?', 'Do you guys have McDonalds?', 'Are you a Republican or Democrat?'. Twenty-eight pairs of eyes assessed me from every angle, and at the same time I curiously sought to find out more about them.

By the end of the day a picture began to emerge of their personalities. For example, there was Roger, the natural leader in the room, a fast-talking, good-looking football fan who tried to avoid schoolwork at all costs. In stark contrast was Cindy, a quiet and hardworking academic leader who seemed to have everyone's respect because she did everything well. There was also Chanda, a loud girl who liked rock music played at top volume on a ghetto blaster, but who rarely completed schoolwork. And Stephen, who seemed to be at war with the world.

Jean had invited me into her classroom to help implement a new 'whole language' curriculum. She had a sound knowledge of language and learning developed through her undergraduate and masters programs, but felt she needed help to implement the ideas which reflected her own philosophy. Jean believed that language should be taught holistically and that children should be in control of their learning. And yet, in Jean's initial weeks in the classroom, she had developed a reliance upon set texts. Her day was divided into clearly defined subject times, and she taught the class as a single group.

When I arrived in her classroom — in the third week of semester — her language program consisted of compulsory journal writing for the first ten minutes of each day (this was a school initiative and was motivated by the desire to 'settle children down' each morning), spelling from a set text, some formal language lessons which were given as the need arose (e.g. using quotation marks), basal reading for twenty minutes per day (all students on the one level), and writing based primarily on imposed topics.

Jean's program in these early weeks had been strongly influenced by other teachers and her principal. Their advice had emphasised the use and reliance on textbooks. But Jean wanted her children to see the generative potential or openness of language, and she realised that this was not possible if she continued to teach with total reliance on materials. She wanted her students to become risktakers and to assume full control of their learning, but she agonised over the fact that her children were not developing a thirst for learning.

However, while these children showed little commitment to school literacy tasks, they frequently used literacy for their own purposes, as part of the network of relationships present within their classrooms. I found that notes were passed, posters were designed advertising a Cabbage Patch Kid club, signs were posted on desks warning others to leave things alone (or risk 'broken faces'), joke books were shared, music was read (and enjoyed), the words from a favourite piece of rock music were copied, magazines were shared, and so on. Reading and writing were being used for functional purposes, but only outside the school curriculum (Cairney 1987b).

## 3. A year one in the south west of NSW

When I first walked into Inta's classroom (a grade one in a small Christian community school) I was struck by the 'busyness' of it, both physically (see floor plan below), and in terms of pupil behaviour. It was also at times messy and noisy, but always there was an atmosphere of work and engagement in a variety of tasks.

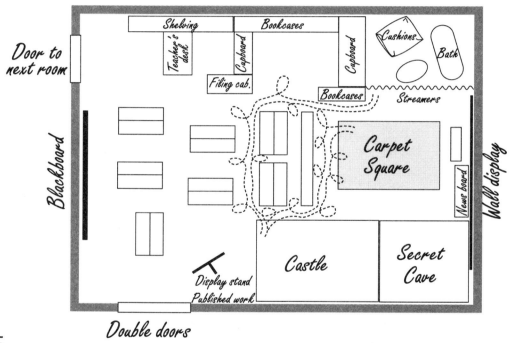

Floor plan of Inta's classroom

The first day I entered the children had already started working. The following extract from my field notes (recorded during and at the end of my first visit) provides a record of my initial impressions:

As I entered the room there was activity everywhere. Children were sitting at desks writing, writing folders were lying open revealing masses of twisted, trampled paper — drafts as yet unpublished. Several children were sitting discussing something, perhaps their stories. Inta didn't realise I'd entered the room at first. Finally, someone caught her attention, and mentioned that I was there. She smiled, walked over, said hello and asked me what I wanted to do. I replied that I was happy to wander around talking and helping if needed.

The children seemed to work on in spite of me watching and peering. No-one asked what I was doing there. Everyone seemed prepared to let me observe them. In fact several seemed thrilled to have my prying eyes looking at their work, writing a word, looking up to smile, writing another and so on. The independence with which they worked is reflected in the following field note entry:

> Shortly after 10.00 a.m. a visitor arrives from next door asking if the class will be coming for the regular television program. Inta announces: 'If you'd like to go next door for TV put your folders away and go on through. If you'd like to keep writing then just keep on going.' Several children drop everything and run, others finish the word or sentence they're on and make their way next door. Eleven students keep working on, while the rest leave over a period of ten minutes.

As I spent time in this classroom it became clear that these five- and six-year-old children were remarkably self-directed. As I wandered around on the first day two girls were lying on the floor writing, two more were inside a 'magic cave', another three were in a 'castle' (both constructed by the class). Several boys were looking at encyclopaedias in search of information on snakes and lizards. Everywhere there was a gentle hum of noise which rose to a roar at times only to be gently lulled by Inta. These children were involved in literacy because it was significant to them.

## Interpreting these Vignettes

The classrooms described are living evidence of the complex social nature of literacy. In Inta and Susan's classrooms members of the class are talking, listening, reading and writing as parts of a dynamic community. Literacy is being learned as children relate to each other, meaning is being created within a complex community of relationships. In Jean's classroom we see the same thing happening, but this time outside the confines of the legitimate curriculum. The children have created their own underground network of literacy contacts. They have created their own sub-culture that values and shares literacy but which excludes the teacher. These three classrooms demonstrate many of the social elements of literacy I will explore in other parts of this book, and which are of great importance for teachers of literacy.

Reading and writing are inherently social. A concern for the social nature of literacy should lead to a recognition that reading and writing events involve relationships. Bloome (1985, p.134) suggests that:

> ...reading involves social relationships among people: among teachers and students, among students, among parents and children, and among authors and readers. The social relationships involved in reading include establishing social groups and ways of interacting with others; gaining or maintaining status and social position; and acquiring culturally appropriate ways of thinking, problem-solving, valuing, and feeling.

Children need to be introduced to the world of literacy in an environment where it is valued. Reading and writing should be shared and enjoyed, as an extension of close relationships (teacher-to-child, child-to-child). The interactions we permit and encourage in our classrooms make a big difference to the literacy development of our students. The way we organise our classroom physically (grouping arrangements, provision or non-provision of communal workspaces), the way we control interactions (e.g. do we insist on children raising hands whenever they speak, do we allow movement in the room?), the role we play in the classroom (are we participants/learners, or directors and teachers?), all make a difference to the learning that occurs. Issues such as these are just as important as decisions concerning teaching methods (Cairney 1987a).

The social context of the classroom has a powerful effect on the beliefs children hold about literacy. All teachers need to acknowledge the role they play in this social context. Sadly, some children live within school contexts in which literacy learning is primarily seen as a teacher-centred, textbook-dominated activity. Reading and writing are seen simply as school subjects (Cairney 1987a). Bloome (1985) claims that if children are asked to do the same low-level task lesson after lesson, month after month, grade after grade, that they may develop a set way of seeing and doing reading and writing.

Evidence from Susan and Inta's classrooms suggests that if one creates an environment in which literacy is an important part of the children's world, that it has a strong positive effect upon literacy development. Susan and Inta's children are learning that reading and writing are used to communicate and share with others, and that they are a functional part of life. Within Jean's classroom, the students are learning something quite different. The curriculum the teacher has planned is reinforcing for these children that schooling (and specifically school literacy) is not relevant to their world, in spite of the fact that within their world, literacy already has a place. Jean's curriculum is serving simply to alienate children from the mainstream curriculum. Unlike the students in Susan and Inta's classrooms, they are not learning that reading and writing are purposeful vehicles for learning. Nor do they see literacy as natural and pleasurable extensions of their social world.

The aim of this book is to try to help teachers redress the problems of classrooms like Jean's. It is a book about literature, but it is not simply an ideas book. It doesn't set out to provide simple recipes. Rather, it is an attempt to show teachers how they can create communities of avid readers, sharing and learning together as a natural extension of their personal worlds. Of vital importance to the creation of these communities is the return of literature to a position of prominence in the school curriculum. Literature is not and should not be seen as a frill. Rather, it should represent the very heart and soul of the language curriculum. This book is not concerned with reading and writing generally, but with literary reading, that is, a personal reading of a text. This reading leads to the creation of one's own representation of the meaning the author wished to convey. It is never exactly the same as any other reader's text, it is highly subjective and individual. I will return to this concept in chapter 2.

I believe that by placing literature at the centre of our programs we can create a stimulating, literate environment. As Nancie Atwell (1984) puts it:

> ...a place where people read, write and talk about reading and writing...where everybody can come inside.

The purpose of this book is to describe the classroom environment and programs that I use to create such a place. It should not be assumed that what I am advocating in this book is a literacy curriculum based entirely upon literary reading and writing. Clearly, the reading and writing of non-literary texts is very important. However, a full discussion of non-literary texts is beyond the scope of this book.

The chapters that follow attempt to show how you can transform a group of reluctant and passive readers into a vibrant group of avid readers. In chapter 2 I discuss what Rosenblatt (1978) means by 'the lived through experience' of books and outline a transactional view of the reading process. As well, I outline the changes necessary if literature is to become an important part of children's worlds. Why is it important to share books? What are the unteachable reading lessons that children learn as we read to them, and they read for themselves?

In chapter 3 the importance of response to literature is examined. What are the forms response can take, and what are the reasons for encouraging it? Finally, I discuss the ways teachers can provide opportunities both for spontaneous and structured response.

In chapter 4 a detailed description is provided of the teacher's role in stimulating the enjoyment of literature. How do we get our children reading regularly? How do we build up a love of literature? As well as describing traditional approaches like Sustained Silent Reading (SSR), this chapter attempts to answer some of the more difficult practical questions. For example, How do we instill a love of books in children who have no books in their homes? How do we get started? How do we monitor children's progress? Should we keep records, and if so, what form should they take? I also describe how group and individual reading conferences and sharing circles can be introduced. How should the teacher set up conferences? How regularly should they be given? What questions do we ask as teachers? What is a 'sharing circle'? Why is it important? How do we introduce them to our classes?

Chapter 5 begins with a challenge for teachers to examine the assumptions that guide instructional practices. It then discusses the features that characterise a literate community — a place where students can read, write and talk about reading and writing. What is the teacher's role in such a classroom? What place does literature assume? What are the components of a literate environment? How can programs be developed that provide for structured response to literature?

Chapter 6 is basically a discussion of approaches and principles for programming. In this chapter I attempt to describe the way teachers can create classrooms which permit literature to be analysed, criticised, assessed, interpreted, compared, and linked with personal knowledge and experiences.

In chapters 7 to 17 I share programs that I have used to encourage literary growth in my classrooms. Finally, in chapter 18 I will conclude this discussion of literary reading with a few final thoughts and warnings.

# The Lived Through Experience of Books

**CHAPTER TWO**

In the previous chapter I argued that as teachers we need to create classrooms where literature is a significant part of group life. In this chapter I want to explore the notion that literature needs to be significant for individuals. In short, I want my students to have a 'lived through experience' of books. Such a statement might evoke a variety of responses. Some might question whether it is simply a romantic notion of little consequence. What do I mean by 'lived through experience'? Is it necessary? These and other questions will be addressed in this chapter.

## What is Meant by a 'Lived Through Experience' of a Book?

Far too many of the students we see in our classrooms are mechanical and passive readers. They see themselves as 'consumers' faced with the constant question: 'What can I get out of these words?' Such an approach to reading is usually adopted by readers who intuitively view reading as:

a) A process of meaning transfer — they assume that meaning resides in a text, and that their job is to try and extract it. That is, to transfer it from the page to their heads.

b) A process of discovering the finite meaning of a text — they assume that good readers all arrive at an identical meaning for a specific text.

c) A precise process depending upon total accuracy when decoding print.

Readers who intuitively view reading in this way:

- read slowly
- spend large amounts of time decoding specific unknown words
- rely on grapho-phonic strategies and fail to use other meaning-based strategies, e.g. read on, leave it out, re-read the sentence and so on

- frequently fail to construct meaning beyond the sentence and paragraph level
- have a task orientation towards reading — they see reading as something to be done for utilitarian purposes, as only a means to an end.

Louise Rosenblatt (1978) has defined the latter (a task orientation) as 'efferent reading'. She suggests that it is a legitimate form of reading and in fact is essential for some reading purposes. Clearly, when reading to assemble a garden shed, cook a meal, or obtain facts about a topic of interest, we need to adopt an efferent approach to reading. We read to get the job done, to complete the task. However, Rosenblatt suggests that at the other end of the continuum we have 'aesthetic' reading. This type of reading is experience-based and requires the reader to relate more closely to the text, to get 'inside' it, to actually live through the story.

Saxby (1987, p. 6) suggests that the 'experience' of literature involves exploration, the reader wanders around inside the story as if 'trying on roles, predicting outcomes' and even 'retreating when necessary'. Literature provides a source of vicarious experiences, 'firing the imagination with sensory and emotive images to provoke imagined experience'. Books arouse the senses and emotions, enrich language and lead to growth in knowledge, social values, ethics, and the human spirit.

Most avid readers are aware what the expression 'to be lost in a book' means. It is this type of experience of reading that leads to the vicarious experiences to which Saxby refers. Many teachers who have created classrooms where literature is a significant part of the classroom world will testify that specific books can have a dramatic impact on a class. I can well recall reading Margaret Davidson's biography *Louis Braille* (1971) to a grade six class which sat spellbound and pleaded to be read just one more page. Students wept openly as we read of Louis Braille's tormented last days struggling for life. They also reacted with anger and frustration as he faced one setback after another in his quest to invent a blind alphabet. This class was empathising with characters, creating images, projecting their own experiences and relationships into the story, in short, living through the book.

It is my contention that many children who read are permanent efferent readers. They read literary texts in a similar way to other texts requiring an efferent approach. Work in the area of comprehension monitoring supports this viewpoint (see Wagoner 1983). This research has shown many readers are so preoccupied with simply getting the words right, they will read a phrase or sentence of complete nonsense (deliberately placed in the text) and not even notice. I believe this type of passivity is at the heart of many children's reading problems.

The avid reader is active, allowing text and self to tussle and merge, constructing meaning, and allowing self to be moulded as part of the complex and dynamic mental trip that reading permits.

Many of our children need to experience literature for the first time. Yes, they have been read literature, yes they have had SSR, but, have they had the experience of really living through a book? Have they felt self merge with characters as they entered the land of Narnia; as they watched Sounder gunned down in cold blood; or, as Rat, Toad, Mole and Badger burst in upon the weasels occupying Toad Hall? Have they ever moved 'inside' a book? (Cairney 1987a)

It might well be argued that students who have not had aesthetic experiences of reading have not read literature at all. A literary text, in a sense, is one which we read as literature. That is, 'literariness' relates to reading practices as much as it relates to the form of the text.

## A Transactional View of Reading

Rather than viewing reading as a process of meaning transfer, we need to recognise it as a constructive process. Such a conceptualisation of reading recognises that:

a) Readers create meaning as a result of transactions with texts.

b) The meaning readers create as they read is 'greater than' the written text's potential meaning, and the reader's prior knowledge.

c) No two readers ever read the same text in the same way; nor do they arrive at the same meaning.

d) Repeated encounters with the same text result in the creation of different meaning for each reading.

e) Above all, meaning is relative — there is no single meaning for any one text.

The reading of a literary text is in effect a dialogue between a reader and a writer, the written text being the vehicle permitting this exchange to occur. This dialogue has the potential for limitless meanings (Bakhtin 1929). The writer's text is riddled with 'blanks' left to evoke the reader's creative participation (Iser 1978). Fox (1979) describes these gaps as a kind of reflective middle ground, a place where reader and text meet.

The writer's written text consists of signs which are given meaning by the reader. It is the act of taking possession of the written text which enables the reader to 'experience' or live through the piece of literature. By this I mean that the reader constructs his/her own text using the signs laid down by the author, and in turn relates these to the sum total of his/her knowledge and experience. The act of reading should lead to a text which belongs to the reader, because it is part of him/her. Readers make texts their own through the meanings they create.

It is important to highlight the fact that I continually use the words *'construct'* or *'create'* to describe the act of reading. Some writers speak of the reader as 'co-creator' or 're-creator' (e.g. Rosenblatt 1978). The difference between the terms 'co-creator', 're-creator' and 'creator' is basically a difference in the way writers apportion responsibility for meaning between the reader and the text. I use the terms 'construct' or 'create' because I wish to emphasise the role that the reader assumes in the reading process. Writers create texts and represent them through a set of signs which readers then use to create their own texts. To suggest that readers 'co-create' implies the writer is involved in the individual reader's construction of a text. This is not the case, the writer simply provides the raw material from which the reader fashions his/her own meaning.

If one accepts this, and the arguments I have developed so far, then there are a number of important implications for classroom teachers. As teachers of reading our priorities should be to:

• help children create more elaborate texts as they read
• support readers as they work at making meaning, not provide isolated skills lessons
• invite responses to texts, not set 'closed' reading activities
• encourage children to make connections between what they know and what they are discovering as a result of a new textual experience.

In short, I am arguing for the creation of classrooms in which reading, sharing and responding to quality literature is an important part of everyday experience.

Like Rosenblatt, I believe that aesthetic reading is important. Not only is it the only way readers can experience a love of reading, it is the only way they can discover that reading is more than simply a process of meaning transfer. As well, it is through the aesthetic reading of texts that readers can receive the many unteachable reading lessons that cannot be received any other way.

I frequently ask readers to tell me why they find the story *The Paper Bag Princess* (Munsch 1980) amusing and enjoyable. They invariably reply that it is because this fairy tale is unlike most others. The prince, named Ronald (!), is carried away by a dragon. Princess Elizabeth goes to rescue him and outsmarts the dragon with cunning (instead of using brute force). She rescues Ronald only to be abused for looking untidy, and so Princess Elizabeth tells him he is a 'toad', and fails to marry him.

I then ask readers of this story how they learned the conventions for fairy tales. They soon realise they built up this great mass of knowledge about language and narrative structure as they heard and read stories. These 'unteachable reading lessons' (Meek 1988) were received as part of the act of reading itself, they were not given by reading teachers.

As well, the aesthetic experience of reading literary texts has other benefits. Einstein observed that Nobel Prize winners and pre-school children asked the same questions, and also made sense of their respective worlds through insatiable curiosity and constant inquiry (McVitty 1986). Aesthetic reading is all about asking questions, of limitless meanings, of open texts and reading tasks. Above all else, it can feed the insatiable curiosity of which McVitty speaks.

Books take their readers into imaginative worlds where all things are possible — they keep children asking questions. For this reason, when Einstein was approached by a mother seeking advice about reading material for her highly intelligent child, he simply replied: 'Give him fairy tales' (McVitty 1986).

Bettelheim's (1976) work has also shown that the aesthetic reading of literature (specifically, fairy tales) can offer symbolic images for the solution of problems like jealousy, discrimination and hatred. In short, they can help readers deal with the inner problems of humanity.

We need to provide children with a rich diet of imaginative literature. All children need to read texts aesthetically, to live through the stories they encounter.

## Making Literature an Important Part of the Classroom World

In classrooms where aesthetic reading is encouraged, literature becomes an important part of the social context. Children not only read books, they talk about them. They share special titles with others. Books that have been shared become part of the common ground which is shared. Parts of books may even find their way into a type of underground curriculum. Keifer (1983) calls this a 'grapevine' response.

For example, *The Very Hungry Caterpillar* (Carle 1981) is passed around from one five-year-old to another until all have discovered the holes through the pages for themselves. Five-year-old children introduce each other to the spiral spider web in *Aranea* (Wagner 1979) and the joy of tracing their fingers around its complex lines. Grade six girls create a new book club so that all members of the group can pool their *Baby-Sitters Club* books. (Martin 1986) for borrowing — to make sure not one is missed in the series. Grade eight students secretly pass around a tattered copy of Judy Blume's *Forever* (1975) and grade two boys share the special secret of the Iron Lady's gigantic (and explosive!) breasts (see *The Tin-Pot Foreign General and the Old Iron Woman*, Briggs 1984).

Books become so much a part of the world of these classrooms that members sometimes create secret codes (Cairney 1987a). For example, as the noise rises in my Grade two classroom I turn to the class and say 'I'll eat you up!' This famous line from *Where the Wild Things Are* (Sendak 1988) is a secret code which amuses them, but at the same time warns them to settle down.

Our aim as teachers must be to create environments where books become a natural and significant part of the interactions which take place between students. Our classrooms must be places where talk about books emerges spontaneously as part of day to day activities — venues for 'literary gossip'.

Nancie Atwell (1984) uses a dining-room table metaphor to describe such an environment. She suggests that her dining-room table is the place where she meets with others to 'analyse, criticise, assess, interpret, compare and link books with...knowledge and experiences and generally get inside written language'. Our classrooms need to mirror some of the qualities of dining-room tables. They need to be places where students can share openly, spontaneously, enthusiastically and reflectively.

One of the things that happens in classrooms where this type of environment is created, is that the number of connections made between different texts increases. Readers and writers make links between texts that are written and read (Cairney 1987d). Barthes (1975) argues that no language is original; texts are a variety of writings which blend and clash. All texts are created from the shadows of other texts which form the backdrop of our literary experiences.

As part of a recent research project I visited a grade one classroom regularly for almost six months. The teacher in this classroom (Inta) had an environment in which the sharing of texts written and read was an important part of the students' world. Within this community of readers (described in chapter 1) one frequent observation was that students made connections between the texts they wrote and read. For example, the teacher's reading of Enid Blyton's book *The Enchanted Wood* (1939) was the stimulus for no fewer than ten stories by students. One student continued her 'Faraway Tree' piece for six months (Cairney 1988c).

It is clear that no literary text is written or read in a vacuum. The mental trip that readers make is not only shaped by the culture out of which it has grown, and in which it is encountered, but by a myriad of texts that represent the reader's literary history.

## Helping Children to Become 'Insiders'

What does all this mean? Put quite simply, if we want to develop a class of avid readers, we need to do more than teach them some reading skills, provide materials, prime background knowledge, and so on. Our role as teachers is to help readers become 'insiders' (to use Nancie Atwell's term). Much of what is done in the name of reading instruction in classrooms is little more than concern for the mechanical process of reading.

We need to ask ourselves: 'What are my children learning about literacy from my reading and writing programs, the curriculum materials I use, my example and attitude, the priorities I exercise in a typical day?' As teachers, we need to recognise that there is a price to pay for using those basal readers which contain poor quality stories, for relegating literature to the last five minutes of the day, for not being readers and writers ourselves, for only ever stressing the need for accurate oral reading, for organising our classroom so that reading and writing are always seen as 'school subjects'. The price is the creation of young readers and writers with dysfunctional notions about literacy (Cairney 1987a).

Most avid readers can remember at least one book which had a significant impact at some time in their literary pasts. We can recall a book we read right through, and which we loved. Many of us loved our special book so much we read it many times, and for most of us this was a turning point in our reading lives. We had discovered just how powerful and enjoyable reading could be, we had entered a book and become 'insiders' for the first time. For me, that book was *20,000 Leagues Under The Sea* by Jules Verne (1954). I discovered this book as an eight-year-old and read it not once but many times. I lived through the sights and sounds of the mysterious monster from the deep, and felt the fear of the crewmen as they waited for the sickening crunch of metal against the timber of their ship. I smelt the luxurious leather of Captain Nemo's magnificent cabin, and marvelled at his creative genius. I lived through this book in a way that I had never done before.

Some students leave primary school without having read a single book which has been significant for them. For them, reading has been a sea of 'Digger' dogs, dull and dreary trips to the farm, and excruciatingly painful sessions of oral reading in their classrooms. Some have still not had a significant reading experience by the time they leave secondary school. Thomson (1987) found that the reluctant readers he met in secondary school all shared one thing in common; they had school reading histories dominated by phonic-based readers and skills-based approaches to instruction.

One of our major tasks as teachers is to develop readers who take conscious delight in literature (Early 1960). An important factor in achieving this is to encourage students to share responses to literature with others. If a community of readers and writers is to be created, then members of the group must learn to share insights and discoveries about the books they are reading. In chapter 3 I will look closely at response to literature. What is reader response, and why is it important?

# CHAPTER THREE

# Response to Literature

In chapters 1 and 2 it was suggested that response to literature is important. But what do we mean by response, and why is it important? For the purposes of this discussion, response is defined as any observable behaviour which follows, and is directly related to, a specific reading. Such responses can be either structured (and encouraged) by teachers, or unstructured and spontaneous. This definition is sufficiently broad to permit a range of behaviours to be classified as legitimate responses. For example, a sigh, tears, a book report, a verbal comment, a dramatic presentation, a drawing, laughter, re-reading and so on, are all recognisable responses.

Many attempts have been made to classify the range of responses that readers generate. For example, Thomson in his excellent book *Understanding Teenagers' Reading* (1987) identifies six types of response:

a) unreflective interest in the action,

b) empathising,

c) analogising,

d) reflecting on the significance of events and behaviour,

e) reviewing the whole work,

f) consciously considered reflections upon the relationship with the author, textual ideology, understanding of self, and one's reading process.

But while such attempts are worthwhile, they invariably fail to cater for the complexity of response. Very rarely can a single response be classified under one of these unitary labels.

It is almost impossible to judge how one would classify the many types of spontaneous responses (e.g. laughter). Even the more structured responses (e.g. written responses), invariably end up falling into more than one category. Even more futile are attempts to suggest a developmental sequence for these responses. While research like Thomson's has shown specific types of response are observed more frequently with growing reader maturity, it is claiming too much to suggest a specific developmental sequence.

An alternative, and potentially more useful exercise, is to classify the type of mental activity in which readers engage (e.g. Corcoran, in Corcoran & Evans 1987). One of the strengths of this approach is it concentrates on the activity of the mind, rather than the product of the mind's activity. The product (or response) is only of interest because it reflects conscious engagement in the processing of text. Corcoran identifies four basic types of mental activity involved in aesthetic reading:

a) Picturing and imaging — building up a mental picture. Readers picture the scenes of a book as if they are actually there.

b) Anticipating and retrospecting — the mind running a little ahead or behind the point at which the reader has reached in the text. Readers anticipate and hypothesise about upcoming events, or reflect.upon the text they have been creating.

c) Engagement and construction — close identification with the text. Readers become emotionally involved in the text, identifying with characters and situations.

d) Valuing and evaluating — making judgements about a text. Readers make judgements about the worth of the text but also apply their own value judgements to the events and situations that unfold.

One of the greatest advantages of Corcoran's classification is that it raises awareness of the type of processes in which readers engage, without attempting to classify each response. While one could make comments about the likelihood of observing these mental activities at specific maturity levels (and Corcoran does), this is unnecessary and far from useful.

Readers at all levels of reading maturity will engage in these mental activities. All readers for example engage in picturing and imaging. However, the extent to which this mental activity is used will vary depending on the reader's

• engagement with the text
• breadth of related intertextual experiences
• relevant prior experiences
• reading purpose
• immediate context within which the text is read
• ability to decode the print.

Furthermore, readers may often use a number of these activities in a single act of reading. For example, while engaged in picturing and imaging, a reader may be engaging more fully in the text, anticipating what will happen next, and evaluating the worth and interest of the plot as it unfolds. The reading process is quite idiosyncratic with meanings being generated and modified constantly.

Recently, I read *The Quinkins* (Trezise & Roughsey 1978) to a group of second year primary education students. This Aboriginal legend tells of the Imjin Quinkins, creatures that steal children and take them back to their mountain homes. While reading the book out loud to my students I was struck by the author's reference to two willy-wagtails who were watching as Warrenby and Margara searched for their children who had disappeared. I had reached a point in the book where the text reads:

Warrenby said to Margara, "Here are the tracks of the hunting party. We will look about for the tracks of our children." The two willy-wagtails sat and watched. After a long search Margara said, "Now we are certain the Imjin are trying to steal our children."

I stopped the reading, showed the illustration, turned to the group and started to say, 'Isn't that interesting, I wonder if that's where we get the saying "a little bird told me"?' Before I got to 'interesting', a student said, 'Yeah, it's just like *Picnic at Hanging Rock*.'

At the moment I inferred the willy-wagtails had told the children's parents what had happened (something not stated explicitly in the text), one of my students was deeply involved in the creation of her own image of the scene. My response was deeply rooted in childhood memories of a school principal who constantly suggested that a little bird had told him something. My student's, on the other hand, was linked with an experience of a film. Not only does this example show how idiosyncratic our responses are, it shows how the same set of words on a page can lead to readers engaging in quite different mental processes.

Quite clearly, any reading act leads to a range of responses, each of which has the potential to change the meaning the reader has constructed as part of the act of reading.

## Why is Reader Response Important?

The above discussion addressed the question, What is reader response? But why is response important? Why should we encourage our students to respond to literature? I would like to suggest that there are five major reasons:
1. Response is a natural consequence of reading and should never be suppressed.
2. Response allows the reader to re-evaluate his/her lived through experience of a text, and reflect upon the text that has been created as an outcome of the reading.
3. Response is essential to help build the common literary ground which binds a community of readers together.
4. Readers learn as a consequence of being party to the responses of other readers.
5. Response permits the teacher to make judgements and predictions about the students' reading processes.

In the rest of this chapter I expand each of these points more fully.

### 1. Response is a natural consequence of reading and should never be suppressed

In chapter 1 I argued that reading is a socially constituted human activity. As such, it occurs within a rich social context as an extension of relationships and the culture of the group. It is inevitable therefore that response is a natural consequence of reading. Because we read for social reasons, (e.g. to establish common ground with someone we see as important to us), we naturally wish to share our reading with others.

In fact, I would argue that response is the inevitable consequence of almost every encounter with a text. I qualify my statement by saying 'almost every encounter' because there are times when a reading is so disturbing or moving that we cannot share a response. For example, after finishing *Bridge to Terabithia* (Paterson 1987a) I wasn't able to speak to anyone for hours because it had such an emotional impact on me. Nevertheless, later I was able to share my response with others.

I should add another qualification — not all responses are to be shared. Clearly there are some responses to a book which are not intended to be shared with others. I can vividly recall sitting in a light aircraft cruising at 9000 feet having just finished Betsy Byars' book *The Pinballs* (1977). After what must have been a period of five to ten minutes I became aware that I was clutching the book tightly in my hands with my hands between my knees. I was simply smiling and reflecting upon the text, and in particular, Carlie, the central character. The warmth of my response was not meant for anyone else, it was a spontaneous result of the lived through experience of the book.

Nevertheless, many responses are meant to be shared. We want to share the joy, pain, fear, frustration, anger, warmth, indifference...that has resulted from a specific reading experience. It is important that we allow this to occur. We need to develop an environment in which students feel free to share these responses with the teacher and each other. In fact, this is a vital factor in the development of a community of readers.

## 2. Reader response allows one to re-evaluate (re-live) the experience of a text

Iser (1978, p. 67) describes reading as a dynamic process of self-correction which involves '...a feedback of effects and information throughout a sequence of changing situational frames; smaller units constantly merge into bigger ones, so that meaning gathers meaning in a kind of snowballing process'. In other words, an aesthetic reading of text depends on the reader's preparedness to revise the text he/she is constructing in memory. The reader's prejudices, background experiences, prior knowledge, intertextual knowledge and so on, all help to shape the text as it is read.

Response enables readers to reflect upon the details of the text they are constructing in memory. Furthermore, the very act of response will lead to changes to the text in memory. As well, having the opportunity to listen to the responses of others, and to have them react to one's interpretations, leads to revision and reshaping of the text.

In the chapters to follow, the comment is frequently made that it is the opportunity to share responses rather than the quality of responses, which is all-important. This underlying assumption shapes many of the lessons planned in the programs in this book.

### 3. Response is essential to help build common literary ground

Reading as stressed in chapters 1 and 2 is a social activity. As such, it is primarily something which humans need to share. For centuries shared meanings from literature have been part of the common cultural ground which shapes our thinking and behaviour.

There are some who would claim literature as the saviour of society as *they* know it, who would argue that a reading of the classics is essential for 'preserving all that is important'. While I have some problems with this romantic and somewhat elitist position, I do believe that literature permits members of a social group to establish common ground. Books do permit members of a group to share common knowledge, beliefs and values. For example, a class that has shared the reading of Heide's book *The Shrinking of Treehorn* (1979) might silently chuckle as their school principal announces during assembly that his job is 'to guide the members of his team', and that he is always there to help with problems. They will inevitably associate the words of their principal with the words of Treehorn's principal who was of no use when he was shrinking. This class will be party to understandings that people who have not shared in the experience of this book will miss.

Books expand our world. As a class shares books, the individual world of each child is affected, and the common ground shared by all grows (Cairney 1987a).

### 4. Readers learn as a consequence of being party to the responses of other readers

A consequence of the belief that reading is a constructive process, is that members of the same social group will inevitably share insights and understandings for any literary text that is read. Because we share common values, experiences and knowledge, we will share common elements within the texts we construct as we read. However, there will be many differences as well, and it is the sharing of these differences which will lead to the expansion of the reader's understanding of the text's meaning.

In recognising this fact Bleich (1978) suggests that literary interpretation is in fact a 'communal act', it is not an individual act at all. A class group has a social authority and an aggregate of values which influence the 'subjective criticism' (interpretation) of any text. Bakhtin (1929) suggested that language use is always subject to the operation of two distinct forces. Centrifugal forces are at work and lead to the production of multiple meanings as the speaker, reader or writer brings his/her own knowledge, experiences and prior textual encounters to produce unique interpretations. At the same time, centripetal forces are at work as the shared beliefs and experiences of a specific social group lead to conformity to accepted group meanings.

I can vividly recall discussing *Grandpa* (Burningham 1980) with one of my daughters (four years old at the time) after having just read it out loud. I asked her at the conclusion if she liked it. She replied, 'Yes.' I then said, 'Why?' To which she replied, 'I don't know.' Not to be outdone I probed further. 'What was it about?' 'Oh, about a little girl and her grandpa.' 'Oh,' I replied, 'and how did it end?' to which she responded, 'They went away in a boat to Africa.'

Anyone who has read *Granpa* will know that it ends with an empty chair which most interpret signifies the death of Grandpa, and is followed by a page showing a little girl pushing a pram, which most believe signifies that 'life goes on'. My daughter's comment relates to the final page which has written text (before the empty chair). It presumably reflects the little girl's comment 'Tomorrow shall we go to Africa, and you can be captain?' Within the story the reason for this comment is unclear, but it may reflect an excursion into imaginative daydreaming, a reaction to story reading, something on television and so on. However, for my daughter, this comment reflects reality and marks the end of her text.

As an adult I had the option of attempting to exert centripetal forces in the form of my own comments to encourage her to reshape her text. On this occasion I chose not to do this.

However, three years later when an international literature expert Margaret Meek was visiting our home, these forces were exerted. She brought a copy of another Burningham book with her, *Where's Julius?* (1987). When my daughter saw the cover (and noticed the Burningham style) she said, 'We've got another book by John Burningham.' She quickly found *Granpa* and returned. When my wife saw it she said, 'That's a sad book.' My daughter gave a puzzled look and sat down on the floor to re-read it. After several minutes without further comment from the adults she exclaimed, 'Oh, now I can see why it's sad.'

Three years after her first reading of this book her text was dramatically reshaped due to the influence of the 'aggregate' meaning given to this book by other readers. This anecdote shows how readers expand their mental texts as meanings are shared, although most of the time, the adjustments made to one's text are far more subtle and minor than the above example. Nevertheless, the sharing of responses permits readers to reshape meaning.

## 5. Response permits the teacher to make judgements and predictions about the students' reading processes

As indicated earlier in this chapter, the responses that our students make to texts are laden with many potential insights about them as readers. For example, I like to interrupt the reading of *Fair's Fair* (Garfield 1981) at the point where Jackson (an urchin living in dockside London in Victorian times) discovers something attached to a dog's collar. I then ask my students to predict what the object might be. The responses always vary greatly. They include a rock, key, dollar note, pound note, letter, name tag and so on. Each of these responses tells me something about the texts they are creating in their heads, the type of background knowledge they are bringing to this text and so on.

For example, the student who suggests that it is money shows that he is anticipating Jackson will be rewarded with a change of luck later in the story. In turn, the child who says it is a 'pound note' is no doubt aware that this story is set in England, whereas the child who says a 'dollar' is less aware of this fact.

Every response is laden with information about the student's reading of the text. The teacher of literature needs to recognise that this information is valuable data which tells something about the reading processes of students. We need to be sensitive to this, to look for evidence that our students are empathising with characters, evaluating the text, building complex images, predicting what will come next, reflecting upon earlier events, engaging with life situations and so on.

## Providing Opportunities for Response to Literature

Having discussed the importance of response, it is necessary to discuss how opportunities can be provided for response in the classroom. To do this I find it useful to use the separate (but not mutually exclusive) labels *spontaneous* and *structured* response.

### 1. Spontaneous response

The intent of everything which has been said so far in this book has been to lead to the creation of classrooms which not only permit response to literature but encourage it. The first priority of the teacher of reading is to create a classroom environment in which students want to share personal insights about their reading of literature. Time needs to be provided for this to occur. One of our greatest mistakes as teachers is to plan our day's activities so well that informal opportunities are not provided in which children can share.

In my classrooms I try to allow regular free time which can be used to talk about books. The creation of physical spaces within the room where students can mingle will also help this. To encourage this type of sharing I also use a number of simple procedures, I:

- create opportunities for book chats: time for a group of children who have read the same book to talk about it
- provide a 'Great Books Graffiti Board' on which I encourage students to write the names of great books — complete with a simple recommendation
- plan author sharing sessions in which students can share titles, comments, favourite parts and so on
- model the sharing of responses by talking about the books that I have enjoyed.

The emphasis with spontaneous response is that there is no special agenda. That is, students are encouraged to respond when, and if they want to.

## 2. Structured response

The major difference between spontaneous and structured response is that the latter requires more direct teacher involvement in the business of encouraging response. Whereas spontaneous response primarily requires the teacher to provide time, structured response requires the teacher to be more actively involved in stimulating response, inviting students to respond in particular ways, and so on. Often student responses will be a direct result of a situation the teacher has structured, a question that has been asked, and so on.

The programs that follow in this book all consist of lessons designed to encourage students to respond to texts. In these programs the teacher has a major responsibility to create situations which encourage a three-way interaction between a teacher, other readers and a text. It is important to stress that this role must not be one of a captain leading his/her charges to the 'real' meaning locked up in texts. As Margaret Meek (1986) has pointed out, when introducing literature to our students, nothing should ever '...stand between reader and author, for we are parasitic middlemen'. Teachers and students help each other build their own mental texts as a consequence of reading and sharing.

This can be done in many ways. Traditionally, group discussion has played a vital part. Within the programs contained in chapters 7 to 17 the importance of spoken language will be given strong emphasis. However, there will be an attempt to share ideas concerning the use of other ways of making and sharing meanings, for example, drawing, using drama and writing.

Before looking more closely at the planning of these more structured programs, it is important to look at the complete classroom context. Into what type of classroom environment do we introduce programs of this type? What are the essential features of a literature-rich environment? How can a classroom be organised to give literature an important place? What are the respective roles of the teacher and students in such a classroom? These and other questions are the subject of chapter 4.

# Creating a Stimulating Literary Environment

CHAPTER FOUR

Some books on literature-based approaches to literacy give the impression that all that needs to be done to create a literate environment in the classroom is to add books. Let me stress at the outset that it is not this simple. This book is not about offering twenty-minute, short-cut recipes for hassled teachers.

While your classroom is going to be dependent upon a good supply of literature, there are many other things that need to change as well. The purpose of this chapter is to examine some of the issues we need to address as teachers of literacy.

## Uncovering Our Assumptions about Reading

One of the problems we face as teachers is that much of our knowledge is tacit. Each of us operates according to a set of inherent assumptions about literacy, learning and teaching (Hutchings 1985). These assumptions direct our thinking as teachers and influence the type of learning environments we create within our classrooms.

It took me a number of years to realise that literature can be a vital part of the common ground that I am able to share with the students in my classrooms. The turning point came in my second year of teaching while working with a grade six class in the western suburbs of Sydney. I started the year as I had ended the previous one, using school magazines for oral reading, providing comprehension sheets consisting of a passage followed by ten questions (no more, no less), and a battered reading laboratory. However, six weeks into the term I discovered Don Holdaway's latest book (at that time) *Independence in Reading* (1972), which came as part of the very first Core Library produced by Ashton Scholastic. It was presented to me by the principal with the comment: 'I want you to try this out.' Surprisingly, my first action was to read Holdaway's book, rather than simply attempting to use the materials. This publication was to trigger changes in me that transformed my approach as a teacher.

As a direct result of *Independence in Reading* I began to ask my students about their reading — I was to make many discoveries. When I talked to them I found that while they could all read, (although in some cases only just), none of them did. No-one had read a book recently, and most had never read a complete novel. Even the best readers in this class could only recall one or two books they had read through the primary school years. These children could read, and they borrowed books from the school library, but they did not read them. Reading for this class was primarily a school-related phenomenon.

The 100 paperback books which came with the Core Library provided the perfect springboard for dramatic changes in my reading program. Up to this point, reading in my room had been dominated by round robin reading of school magazines, comprehension sheets consisting of a short passage followed by ten questions, and a well-worn SRA reading laboratory.

I began to make changes by introducing an independent reading program. For thirty minutes every day I allowed my students to read books of their choice. I also started scavenging as many pieces of literature as possible to build up a class library. I pleaded with the public and the school librarian for bulk loans, and asked children to bring in their favourite books. A class library was created and my students started to read almost immediately.

I began having conferences with my students to talk about their books (where my role was mainly to listen), and encouraged them to get together to share their literary experiences. As well, I started to provide time for my class to respond in their own way to anything they had read. This took the form of drawing, dramatisation, writing, craft and so on. Finally, I started reading quality literature to them every day. By the end of the year my students had read collectively over 1500 books.

In spite of the almost instant results that were obtained with the injection of literature into my classroom I continued to cling to some of the practices that had dominated my program at the start of the year. For example, I persisted with the periodic use of comprehension stencils and the reading laboratory.

It took nearly a year for me to shed these practices. Why, you might ask. How could I have persisted with practices which ran counter to the philosophy of Holdaway's independent reading program? At the time I was unaware of this anomaly, but it seems clear to me today that while I had introduced literature into my classroom, I was still clinging to a number of *inappropriate assumptions*. Implicitly I was assuming that:

a) Readers do not learn how to make meaning, but rather have to be taught to comprehend.

b) The independent reading of literature students chose themselves was somehow of less value when learning to read than the texts the teacher chose for them.

c) Reading is a process of information transfer — all my students needed to get the same information from a text to show they were learning to read.

d) Reading growth can be fostered by testing the ability to transfer information from a written text to one's head.

As a young teacher I had attempted to change my instruction without a parallel change in my views on the nature of reading and the teaching of reading. At the root of my unwillingness to let go some of my old practices was the implicit belief that reading was a process of meaning transfer. I implicitly viewed it as a complex cognitive process that enables the reader to work out what the book is trying to 'say', that is, to get the meaning from the text. As outlined in chapter 2, this conceptualisation of reading is based on a number of incorrect assumptions. First, that there is one (intended) meaning in the text. Second, that efficient readers are able to extract that meaning. Third, that the efficient reader possesses skills that are necessary to ensure that this transfer takes place.

It takes little imagination to see how these three assumptions led me to continue using comprehension worksheets and the SRA reading laboratory. It took me almost a year to discard these practices and to realize that the literature program that I had implemented had the potential to achieve everything that I had aimed for in my original program. As I did so, I realised that not only had I changed my methods, I had changed the classroom environment as well. I noticed changes in my pupils and in the way I related to them. Prior to the introduction of the literature into the room I had a group of students who after some effort had become an obedient, hard-working, quiet industrious group who rarely got off task. My classroom was a place where:

• people worked quietly
• no-one spoke unless spoken to
• tasks were usually completed alone, or on occasions, in ability groups with set tasks
• students completed what was asked of them
• I marked set tasks and provided feedback in the form of scores, grades and occasionally, written comments.

By the end of the year things had changed. Not only had the curriculum changed, but the environment in which I taught my students had also changed. In this my first year as a teacher who used a literature-based program I had had the opportunity to gain new insights. By observing reading and writing in action, and by talking to my students (rather than *at* them) I had modified my assumptions about language, learning and teaching. Not surprisingly, my classroom had changed dramatically, it was now a place where:

• students talked to each other about their work and their interests
• activities were frequently completed in informal interest or friendship groups

- we frequently shared as a class our reading interests
- I talked with all students about their reading interests
- people recommended books to each other
- students spontaneously responded to their reading in a variety of media, including drama, drawing, writing and discussion.

This class had now formed a community of readers that valued reading and gave it prominence in their world. My students were no longer simply students who read because they had to, they now read because they wanted to. They no longer approached a book as a mass of words to be absorbed, but rather saw it as a key to unlock worlds which as yet were undiscovered.

## What are the Features of a Literary Community?

What this experience within my own classroom taught me, and what I have seen confirmed many times since in other classrooms, is that there are a number of key features which mark the classroom where a community of readers and writers has developed. Interestingly, few of these key characteristics are directly related to methodology. Nevertheless, specific methods are often found in classrooms which assume these characteristics.

### 1. The teacher assumes a new role

In classrooms where teachers strive for a sense of literary community they take on new roles. These roles are often complex. Teachers no longer rely on materials and source books. They do not simply follow a teaching guide or administer a set of worksheets. Rather, these teachers become observers, learners and teachers who are required to act as:

- INFORMATION GIVERS if students are unable to fill gaps left by authors in their texts
- interested LISTENERS when students want to share the excitement of a book
- strategy SUGGESTERS if the existing reading strategies of the child are not working
- SHARERS of insights, successes, problems, pain, and joy experienced from personal reading
- OPINION GIVERS who are willing to provide an intepretation or viewpoint on a book
- INTRODUCERS to new language forms, new authors, new uses for reading, new literary genres
- DEMONSTRATORS of real and purposeful reading
- enthusiastic MEMBERS OF THE 'LITERACY CLUB' (see Smith 1988).

| THE CLASSROOM BECOMES A PLACE WHERE... | THE CLASSROOM CEASES TO BE A PLACE WHERE... |
|---|---|
| **The Learner** ||
| Students learn as extensions of social relationships — partner sharing, response groups, whole class sharing. | Students are frequently asked to learn alone. |
| Spontaneous talk is encouraged about the books they are reading. | Talk is frowned upon, except if directed to the teacher. |
| Students can pursue reading without the pressure of competitiveness or failure. | Pressure, competitiveness, and a fear of failure are common. |
| Students see any activities completed as relevant to their needs and purposes. | Students fail to see the teacher's purpose for setting a task. |
| Students are given varied and frequent opportunities to read for a range of reading purposes. | Students often do not have an opportunity to read for non-task related purposes. |
| **The Teacher** ||
| Students are given help in interpreting their reading. | Students are given help through decontextualised skills activities. |
| Reading activities are a means to an end. | Activities are ends in themselves. |
| Students read because they want to, they are intrinsically motivated. | Students read and write for school-related purposes only. |
| Movement around the classroom is encouraged. | Movement around the room is discouraged. |
| Students are frequently engaged in many different reading-related activities at any one time. | Students are usually only engaged in one activity at any one time. |
| Students are treated like fellow learners and the role of expert is shared depending upon the book, author and knowledge of the book. | The teacher is always the expert — their meaning is the final authority. |
| The teacher supports and responds to student needs for help as part of 'real' literacy tasks. | The teacher decides what help the class requires before the need arises. |

## 2. The environment changes

With new roles comes a new type of classroom which reflects new and clearly articulated theories of language and learning. Old practices and procedures are removed and new ones established.

# A New Role for Literature in the Classroom

Just as a change in theoretical orientation is accompanied by a change in roles for teacher and child, so too, the role of literature changes in classrooms where the major aim is the creation of literary communities. Literature has assumed many varied places within schools in the modern era of mass education. For example, in the Victorian era literature was narrowly defined as 'the classics' and was studied as object, as language which was to be aspired to, as the preserver of society's finest qualities. This elitist notion was essentially a way of preserving culture in exactly the way a small section of society felt it should be defined. It was a way of holding on to that which the aristocracy felt was important.

In this book literature is not viewed as an object with precise meanings and values to which we aspire. Rather, as Bruner (1986) points out, it is a doorway to 'other worlds'. There is not a single world view, a single meaning, to which we should all aspire (see chapter 2). Rather, literature enables all readers to make meaning for themselves. Even if there are meanings fixed within our world 'we transform them in the act of accepting them into our transformed world' (Bruner 1986, p.159). Such a view of literature accepts that all fiction has a place. Literary critics and child readers may judge some books as 'better' literature than others (and such views are valid), but all works have legitimacy. All books have the potential to excite the mind of readers. The 'trashy' romance may seem to hold little of which we value but, it has a place.

Our role as teachers is not to impose our definitions of quality upon readers, rather, it is to help students discover the endless possibilities that literature holds for them personally.

In fact, as argued earlier (see chapter 2) it is the nature of the reading experience itself, rather than the text, that should determine what we class as literature. Literature is that which we read aesthetically. When the reader reads for literary (or aesthetic) purposes then the text they happen to read is defined (for our purposes) as *literature*. In other words, if someone reads an encyclopaedia aesthetically (a difficult task), then this text becomes literature for this reader in this context.

Such a definition of literature places a different set of expectations upon the teacher. While the teacher must still strive to provide readers with a range of literary texts, he/she must equally aim to provide a wide range of literary contexts and reading purposes. As readers encounter texts in different contexts, and read them for widely varying purposes, so too, their reading will vary. Not only does the reader's 'mental trip' vary, but his/her response may change dramatically.

Nevertheless, most aesthetic readings occur when one encounters a piece of narrative prose, poetry or drama. The reading of this literature has many advantages because it:

- teaches about language
- aids the development of writing and reading
- helps the reader to learn about his/her world
- helps readers to learn about self
- provides important common ground for the building of a literary community
- offers endless possibilities for the exploration of 'other worlds' and the creation of meaning.

Within the classroom, the outworking of this complex role for literature can be summarised in five major functions. Our students need time to:

- read books of their choice with the sole purpose of reading for enjoyment
- be read quality literature without a response being expected
- share their reading with others (teacher, peers, family etc)
- respond creatively to their individual reading
- listen to and read literature in larger groups so that it can be analysed, criticised, assessed, interpreted, compared, and linked with their knowledge and experiences.

If we are to provide all of these opportunities and help our students to discover the world of literature, we need to make changes to our classroom reading environments. In the following chapter I will begin to describe the type of environment I believe needs to be created if children are to become active meaning-makers as they engage in aesthetic readings of texts. More specifically I will examine the way we create classrooms dominated by books. Some of the questions addressed include: How do we obtain sufficient books for our children? How can we encourage reluctant readers? Do we help children to choose books? Should we change the physical layout of the classroom? What needs to be done to help all students experience the endless possibilities that literature offers?

# Encouraging Children to Read for Enjoyment and Discovery

CHAPTER FIVE

Every book is in essence a doorway to endless possibilities (Meek 1988). Each book invites the reader to create a secret world of which they can be part. A book provides readers with a chance to create a text in their heads which is an outgrowth of every prior literary experience. As Frank Smith (1978) reminded us a decade ago, children learn to read by reading. While this seems a truism, it is one that is often forgotten. The work of Clay, Alpert, Eder and others (see Cairney 1987a) has shown that one of the most frequently observed differences between the experiences of the successful and unsuccessful readers is that the latter read on average only one third the quantity of written text. One might well ask, is there any wonder that these readers never close the gap between themselves and their more fortunate, avid reading classmates.

As pointed out in the previous chapter, silent independent reading not only provides an opportunity to practise, it is in itself a provider of endless 'reading lessons' (Meek 1988). From their experience of texts, readers learn about:
- the structure of narrative
- the variety of written genres
- the infinite meanings that exist for each page of print
- that words don't always mean exactly what they say (Max wasn't really going to eat his mother up)

and so on.

One of the teacher's most important roles then is to connect children with books. The teacher has a number of elements within the classroom that are under his/her control and which need to be manipulated. But how is this to be done, and what are the key variables that the teacher needs to monitor and modify? Of the many elements to consider, the following are the most significant:
- setting up a class library
- providing reading time

- helping children to select appropriate books
- providing opportunities for students to share their reading with others
- broadening students' reading horizons.
Let me deal with each of these issues in turn.

## Setting up a Library

There has often been debate within schools concerning the desirability of class libraries. Some traditional librarians adopt the attitude that they should be avoided because they discourage the use of school or community libraries.

The desire to possess one's own books is a natural response to positive experiences with reading. Most people, if asked, will be able to recall books which were of such significance to them that they needed to possess them. In the same way, students who have positive experiences of books at school will wish to have ready access to them. Just like Mary in *The Stone Book Quartet* (Garner 1988) we all have a desire to have our own books.

There are other more pragmatic reasons for allowing classes to have a class library:

- class libraries make books more readily accessible
- students are able to share their books from home that have been significant to them
- as a teacher you are able to more easily observe students as they select books — something they do not always do well.

When setting up class libraries the following simple hints might be useful:

a) Create a special corner of the room which is readily identified as the library. I always try to move cupboards or shelving around to create a separate section. I then place a carpet square on the floor, some cushions to lie on, and sometimes even an old lounge chair.

b) Encourage students to bring books from home. All books should be clearly labelled with students' names. (You will be thankful at the end of the year that you have followed this simple procedure.)

c) Try to arrange bulk loans from the school and community libraries (these should be changed regularly). When arranging loans you might choose a variety of titles or systematically select books of specific types (e.g. mystery stories, biographies, adventure stories). You might also choose books by specific authors.

d) For younger children it is sometimes useful to group similar books in plastic book tubs or trays. This enables children to move the books onto the floor, which in turn allows them to choose the books in a more relaxed way.

e) Display books so that the covers of many of them are visible. The spines of books rarely look inviting. It is necessary to change these titles at least weekly.

f) If the money is available, purchase one of the growing number of literature sets available (e.g. Core Libraries or Puffin Packs). The advantage of these sets is that they provide a solid core of good books to start your class library.

While the purpose of this book is to talk about the use of trade books not reading schemes, it would be remiss not to mention that literature-based reading schemes can provide some useful material that is already graded. In the past five years a number of publishers have started to include complete pieces of literature within their schemes. Australian programs like Bookshelf (Scholastic) provide a way to place large numbers of good books into classrooms.

Many of the books included in these programs have been commissioned works from well-known authors. In fact the quality of these books has been recognised by the Australian Book Council, which shortlisted two of the books in Bookshelf for the annual book of the year awards in 1988 and another in 1989. If publishers can ensure a high standard of writers and literature, then these programs could make a worthwhile contribution to the literature program.

## Providing Reading Time

It seems almost unnecessary to stress that children need time to read, but it does need to be stressed. In some classrooms independent reading time is not given the status and importance it deserves. Some teachers seem to feel that independent reading for pleasure is in some way less beneficial for reading development than reading lessons, worksheets, laboratories and so on.

In my classrooms I provide twenty to thirty minutes reading time each day. During this time everyone reads. I like to have this reading at a set time each day so students know when to expect it and can get down to reading with a minimum of direction.

I have found that the best time is just after morning recess as soon as the class returns. I teach my students to enter the classroom and begin reading as soon as they are ready. The only 'problem' I have ever found with this timeslot is that sometimes I have had to battle to keep the students out of the room during recess. One real advantage was that normally when I walked into the room all students were reading.

To ensure that these periods run smoothly I normally apply a few simple rules:
• everyone reads
• the reading should not be related to other subjects
• changing books during reading time should be avoided — book selection is normally done outside reading timeslots
• readers can move to any location within the room (sometimes I let students go outside the room) as long as they do not disturb others

- there should be no talk
- the teacher should read too.

As well as reading in these set times, students are encouraged to read during free time or when other work is completed. In all my classes I expect students to have a piece of current reading at their desk. Reading at home is also encouraged. As students begin to experience the enjoyment of reading at school, most quite spontaneously begin to read at home, much to the amazement of parents.

## Helping Children to Select Appropriate Books

While your students usually know the types of books they like, they sometimes have trouble finding them. Part of the reading teacher's role is to be able to help students select books. One of the essential requirements to be able to do this is to know the books in the class library yourself. There is only one way to do this successfully: read them!

I have found that while some students quickly learn how to select books, others use an indiscriminate *kamikaze* approach. At times it may even be necessary to go to the shelves with specific children and guide their choice. Normally this is achieved by simply asking questions designed to identify their interests. For example: Do you like science fiction? Why not try A *Wrinkle in Time* (L'Engle 1973)? Have you read any books by Betsy Byars? Why not try one?

Helping students in this way is always much easier if you know the interests of your children. I always try to obtain as much knowledge of their interests as possible right at the start of the year. Some of this information is obtained informally, however, I use a reading interest inventory in the first few weeks to provide information quickly. The following is typical of many that I have used:

### A sample interest inventory

### Part A

Answer the following questions in the spaces provided.

1. In my spare time I like to . . . . . . . . . . . . . . . . . . . . . . . . . . . . . . . . . . .

. . . . . . . . . . . . . . . . . . . . . . . . . . . . . . . . . . . . . . . . . . . . . . . . . . . . . . .

2. When I grow up I'd like to be . . . . . . . . . . . . . . . . . . . . . . . . . . . . . . .

. . . . . . . . . . . . . . . . . . . . . . . . . . . . . . . . . . . . . . . . . . . . . . . . . . . . . . .

3. A person I admire is . . . . . . . . . . . . . . . . . . . . . . . . . . . . . . . . . . . . . .

. . . . . . . . . . . . . . . . . . . . . . . . . . . . . . . . . . . . . . . . . . . . . . . . . . . . . . .

4. The thing I like most about school is . . . . . . . . . . . . . . . . . . . . . . . . .

. . . . . . . . . . . . . . . . . . . . . . . . . . . . . . . . . . . . . . . . . . . . . . . . . . . . . . .

5. The thing I like least about school is . . . . . . . . . . . . . . . . . . . . . . . .

. . . . . . . . . . . . . . . . . . . . . . . . . . . . . . . . . . . . . . . . . . . . . .

6. My favourite subject at school is . . . . . . . . . . . . . . . . . . . . . . . . . .

**Part B**

Answer the following questions by circling the face which shows how you feel.

1. When I think about reading at school I feel...

2. When I think about reading at home I feel...

3. When I'm asked to read out loud in class I feel...

**Part C**

Answer the following questions in the spaces provided.

1. My favourite book is . . . . . . . . . . . . . . . . . . . . . . . . . . . . . . . . . . .

. . . . . . . . . . . . . . . . . . . . . . . . . . . . . . . . . . . . . . . . . . . . . .

2. In the last year I've read ☐ books

3. How many books (roughly) are in your house? . . . . . . . . . . . . . . . . . . .

4. I like/don't like reading because . . . . . . . . . . . . . . . . . . . . . . . . . .

. . . . . . . . . . . . . . . . . . . . . . . . . . . . . . . . . . . . . . . . . . . . . .

5. The thing I like most about reading at school is . . . . . . . . . . . . . . . . . .

. . . . . . . . . . . . . . . . . . . . . . . . . . . . . . . . . . . . . . . . . . . . . .

6. The thing I like least about reading at school is . . . . . . . . . . . . . . . . . .

. . . . . . . . . . . . . . . . . . . . . . . . . . . . . . . . . . . . . . . . . . . . . .

## ———— Providing Opportunities for the Sharing of Books

As I stated in chapter 1, reading is a social activity. While we often read alone, we usually have a desire to share the things we read. We do this to:

- provide an emotional outlet for the feelings a book has stimulated (e.g. sadness or anger)
- share positive or negative aspects of the reading experience
- find out how another reader interpreted some aspect of plot, characterisation, language etc.

In each case there is a desire to share because books are an extension of our relationships with other people. They are part of the 'common ground' we share.

As teachers we need to provide opportunities for our students to share their responses to literature. In doing so we need to keep in mind the following basic principles:

- don't ask children to respond if they don't want to
- permit a wide range of responses. Don't assume that there is only one way to respond (e.g. a book report)
- always accept any response as legitimate, unless it contains an error of meaning (e.g. suggesting that the main character in *Charlotte's Web* (White 1952) is a spider named Wilbur). This does not mean that you have to agree with the child's response. However, you need to accept it as the reader's personal response. Allow the reader to modify his/her interpretation in the light of alternative interpretations.

Providing opportunities for response is critical. Furthermore, all responses need to be respected and considered. Far too often teachers judge a student's response as 'wrong' rather than simply recognising it as 'different'. At times student responses are seen as naive comments which need to be discarded as he/she is 'pushed towards' a more 'acceptable' response. It needs to be recognised that many meanings are possible for any text, and for any single reader. In other words, the reader's first response may not represent (in fact it rarely does) his/her final meaning for this text. Response and reflection are a natural part of the generative process that readers use to arrive at text meaning. Bill Corcoran (Corcoran & Evans, eds. 1987) urges teachers to provide 'meaning space' which allows students to provide a provisional, holding response. That is, an early, sometimes tentative response which needs to be made as the reader endeavours to construct a full meaning for the text.

There are many ways in which a teacher can provide opportunities for students to share their responses. The following represent the major contexts I have used for this purpose.

### Individual Conferences

The individual conference is a vital part of any community of readers. It is a time for your students to talk, and for you to listen. It is an opportunity for students to share their joys, frustrations and puzzlements from personal reading. It is a valuable time for the teacher to learn about: students as people, (their likes, dislikes, values, prejudices); the reading ability of students; the reading interests of students; students' reading habits, e.g. how often do they read, have they a favourite author?

In my classrooms I have an interview with each pupil at least once a week. Interviews are always held at variable times (rarely during reading) when I am sure the class can work independently without me. I simply announce that I will have interviews and ask students to write their names on the blackboard if they want to share their reading with me. I then talk to each student in turn either at his/her desk or at mine. Students are not required to have an interview (although in reality they virtually always choose to do so), but I monitor this to make sure that all students are reading regularly.

Each interview lasts approximately two to ten minutes. Students are asked to bring a list of the titles they have read and at least one novel to share. All students keep a record of their reading in a workbook, listing the titles, authors and date completed. The interview usually starts with: 'Tell me about your reading this past week.' This is usually followed by a spontaneous and enthusiastic sharing of the highlights of the books read. After conducting interviews in this way for many years I have found that the following hints are helpful:

- if students continually retell complete books (some children could talk for hours about their reading) gently use specific questions to focus their discussion. For example, tell me why you like the book. What is it that 'got you in'? Who was your favourite character? Why? How is this book different from the last book you read? The aim in asking questions like these is to discourage a complete retelling of the story
- share your own responses to the same book if you've read it
- suggest other suitable titles. Mention other books by the same author
- record the name of each book read on a file card (keep one for each child) and the date completed. This acts as a valuable record of each student's reading and enables you to monitor regularity of reading, the type of books read, popular authors, etc.
- work hard at being a listener. The conference is the child's turn to talk and your turn (primarily) to listen.

**Readers' Circle**

This is essentially an opportunity for group sharing. I use planned and informal readers' circles. Planned readers' circles involve the selection of four to six students for group talk with similar reading interests, or who have read the same book. Usually a set format is followed in these discussions with a nominated leader making sure that the group stays on task.

One format for such a group involves the following steps:

- all group members share the things they liked about the book

- all share the things they did not like
- group members share parts of the book which puzzled them
- group members compare the book with others they have read
- group members recommend further reading for the group.

Informal readers' circles are less structured. Usually they are formed along friendship lines with students forming their own group of four to eight students to discuss a book, comment on an author's style, dramatise a piece of poetry and so on. Sometimes a task is set for the groups but often the students decide how they will use their time to talk about books.

One of the greatest advantages of a readers' circle is that it enables students to share personal insights about reading. This in turn leads to growth as readers. One essential rule for this type of response situation is that group members accept each other's responses, not assuming that there is a single 'correct' interpretation for any piece of literature.

## Class Discussion

In the 1970s with the move towards independent learning the use of whole class lessons was frowned upon. This was unfortunate because using the class group is often a good way to discuss literature. The great benefit of a class group is that you can hear thirty responses to a single piece of literature. Such a large number of responses has the potential to help readers 'stretch their texts'. That is, readers can add to, elaborate and revise the mental texts they have created as they read a specific piece of literature.

As pointed out in chapter 2, no two readers ever create exactly the same texts as they read. Class sharing allows readers to hear alternative explanations and revise their meanings if they feel an alternative explanation is more appropriate.

## Dialogue Journals

Dialogue journals provide another valuable way to share one's reading. Nancie Atwell (1987) is one of many literacy educators who has found that dialogue journals are invaluable when teachers don't have enough time to talk to each student about reading.

Essentially, a dialogue journal is a book kept by each student to record responses to the literature they have been reading. It is usually personal in style and is shared primarily with the teacher and other interested peers. The following entry from a grade eight student is typical of the type of written response entered in the journals.

While the dialogue journal is less personal than an individual conference, it has a number of clear advantages. One of the major advantages is that the teacher can respond to students in the dialogue journals out of class time. This allows the teacher to give a more considered response and can set up a written form of dialogue. Another advantage is that a written response allows the reader to

> Mr C. 6/2/88
>
> I've just finished reading Jacob have I loved by Katherine Paterson. I'm not sure if I'm depressed, angry or confused by this book. Just like in Bridge to Terabithia Paterson builds the tension in the story then hits you with a sledge hammer. Have you read it? How did you feel about the twins? How did you feel about Carolyn? I found myself getting annoyed with her at times. I don't think Louise was near as bad as she thought. Now the grandmother was another story — what a witch! If you've read it let me know, I'd love to talk to you about it, I'm a bit confused by this book.
>
> Sally

reflect upon his/her response to the book as it is written. At times the very act of writing can help the reader clarify the meaning constructed from the experience of reading the book.

## Avoiding the Task Orientation Trap

It is important to end this chapter by stressing that when striving for a literary reading of texts, we must never make changes in the class-room, or introduce procedures which shift the focus from an aesthetic to a task orientation — from a 'lived through experience' to an assign-ment to be completed. This is even more critical when designing programs for the discussion and analysis of literature. This issue will be dealt with in greater detail in the following chapter which examines approaches to programming.

# Programming for Structured Response to Literature

It is the provision of programs which permit literature to be analysed, assessed, interpreted and criticised which constitutes the focus for the rest of this book. In chapters 1 to 5 I have discussed the creation of classroom environments in which literature is read independently, listened to for enjoyment, shared, and responded to, and so on. My primary concern in the chapters which follow is the provision of guidance in the area of structured response to literature. How can we help our students to become 'insiders', living through the book, relating to characters, feeling the tension of the plot, and so on?

To provide a framework for structured response to literature I have adopted a programming approach which has worked for me in a variety of classroom settings. In each case I have selected a book, or a series of books related in some way, and planned lessons to systematically work my way through these pieces of literature. The approach adopted could be loosely called an integrated approach and concentrates on the themes within the novel (i.e. major points that the author has attempted to communicate), plot, characterisation, structure, setting and language. Other approaches are available (although they are not used in this book). These include:

a) Genre (form) approach — which has as its major focus the distinctive features of a particular text genre (e.g. fairy tales, fables, Aboriginal legends and so on). This can provide useful variation to any program.

b) Topic approach — this form requires the teacher to select books by topic, e.g., animal stories. This type of program is less useful because it shifts the emphasis away from the book to the topic.

c) Structural approach — the focus with this type of program is on the plot structure of the text(s). Many stories have a predictable plot structure and can be compared to look for consistency with the 'typical' structure. This type of program has limited use and most of its aims can be achieved in the programs outlined in the rest of this book.

d) Author studies — involve the study of several books by the same writer. The program often begins with the teacher sharing details on the author and is followed by the close reading of a number of books to identify aspects of the author's style. This type of program is of use at regular intervals, or as student interest in specific authors becomes apparent.

## Using an Integrated Approach to Programming

As stated above, the program form I prefer is the integrated program format. Before examining examples of this form it is important to look at the principles that shape the lessons planned. In preparing these programs I attempt to conform to the following principles:

a) The activities planned should never trivialize the meaning that individual readers construct as they read or listen to a piece of literature. For example, when using *Charlotte's Web* (White 1952) it would generally be inappropriate to plan a sequence of lessons about spiders. While there are some wonderful sections describing Charlotte and her activities (e.g. spinning her web) the book is not primarily about pigs and spiders. Rather, it is more concerned with friendship, loyalty, life and death. Of course, if students become fascinated by spiders, allow them to pursue their interests individually.

b) The activities planned should be as open as possible. That is, they should provide opportunities for students to respond in their own way. An open activity is one that permits many responses. A closed activity allows only one response.

c) We should provide invitations to respond, not set tasks. To ensure that there are sufficient activities to achieve this it is often necessary to provide choice, rather than just one set activity.

d) Avoid forced integration when planning lessons. The aim is to plan meaningful language activities which permit our students to come to a greater understanding of the text. Never set out to plan activities for a variety of subjects without regard for the integrity of the book.

e) Above all, provide activities which promote the sharing of alternative responses to the text, avoid the tendency to promote one set meaning for any book.

f) Ensure that activities are only means to the end of encouraging response to the text. Avoid the trap of shifting the focus from the book to the language activities.

But how can the planning process take place? How would I normally make a start to the daunting process of programming? While it is possible to follow a number of procedures when planning such a program, I find that the following steps are useful:

**Step 1** Read the book without taking notes or planning any lessons.

**Step 2** Re-read the book looking for logical divisions or lesson-sized chunks (i.e. sections that can be read in ten to fifteen minutes) and record the page numbers where 'break' points occur.

**Step 3** Skim through the book again section by section, making notes concerning possible lessons that look at the underlying themes, characterisation, plot, setting, language and form.

**Step 4** Go over notes, eliminating less desirable lessons, adding other ideas and so on.

**Step 5** Revise the lesson content, giving consideration to the length of the lesson, the ability and interests of the students and so on.

**Step 6** Prepare a final program with lessons that conform to the above principles.

The format used within the programs may vary, depending upon the specific needs of any teacher, however, the form followed in the rest of the book is one that I have found useful.

The way in which the book is presented to the class may also vary. Each of the programs has been written assuming that the teacher will read the story out loud to the class, however if multiple copies are available, you may have your students read the book themselves. Alternatively, the reading could be part student, part teacher. If necessary, each program could be modified to allow students to read the texts individually, in groups or as a class.

When reading each of these programs it is important to remember that I have planned them with specific students and particular contexts in mind. The programs are not meant to suit all situations and children. As a teacher you need to ensure that the literature program you use:

a) Matches your students' needs. What do they need to learn about literature?

b) Matches your students' interests. What type of books do they enjoy?

c) Stretches your students as language users. What are their greatest needs at this time?


## A final warning

As indicated in the last chapter one of the dangers with this type of programming is that the things we do in the name of literature can very easily move the focus from the literary work to the tasks set. We can so easily make our readers more concerned about information to be carried away or any number of agendas that we inadvertently set. This concern needs to be kept in mind as we consider the programs that follow.

The programs provide examples of the types of lessons I have planned and taught in a range of educational settings. They were used with readers of different ages and feature a wide range of authors and literary styles. They are presented here to provide an insight into the types of lessons that can be planned to foster response to literature. They are not presented as eleven exemplary literature programs.

CHAPTER SEVEN                     # I'll Always Love You

**Literature:**   *I'll Always Love You*, Hans Wilhelm
*Granpa*, John Burningham
*John Brown, Rose, and the Midnight Cat*, Jenny Wagner
**Suggested Level:**   Kindergarten (Prep.) to Grade two

## SYNOPSES

### I'll Always Love You (1985)

This is a story about a boy and his dog. It begins, 'This is a story about Elfie — the best dog in the world'. As Elfie and her young master grow up together a strong bond develops between them. As both age, the way they spend their time together changes, but the bond of love never alters, and seems to remain even after Elfie finally dies one night in her sleep. A touching story that tackles the often avoided theme of death.

### Granpa (1980)

Like *I'll Always Love You*, this book tells the story of two characters bonded together in love, who are finally separated from each other through death. Burningham creates a brilliantly different look at the relationship between a little girl and her grandpa. The story is a series of snippets from their life, the two characters sharing each other's company, but often seeming to be talking about, and doing, different things. A powerful and moving story.

### John Brown, Rose, and the Midnight Cat (1977)

This story once again deals with a strong relationship of love between two characters — Rose and her dog, John Brown. A black cat tries to come between Rose and John Brown. While Rose is prepared to allow it to come between them, John Brown is not. For many readers the black cat will represent just another character competing for Rose's love. However, Jenny Wagner has used the black cat to represent death and the separation that it brings for loved ones. A fascinating book which can be read at many different levels.

## PROGRAM FOCUS

The major purpose in planning this program for the three picture books outlined above is to examine the extent to which each deals with:

- the give and take nature of relationships with special people or pets — those we love
- the theme of death.

To do this opportunities will be given to respond through talking, drawing, writing and drama.

In looking at each of these themes great sensitivity is required, especially in relation to death. Some teachers avoid this theme, however, I believe it is something which we have a responsibility to discuss.

## POSSIBLE LESSONS

### LESSON 1

The purpose of this lesson is to introduce the book *I'll Always Love You* (Wilhelm  1985) and discuss the special nature of relationships we can share with our pets.

**Procedure**

Read the book right through without comment or interruption.

At the conclusion of the reading ask your students the following questions:

- Did you like the book? Why or why not?
- How did it make you feel? Why?

Following this discussion ask your students if they have a special pet, or have had one in the past. What was it? What was its name? Why did they love it so much?

After discussion ask your students to draw their pet, write its name on the sheet and perhaps write something about it.

For very young children (five-year-olds) you might simply ask them to say why they loved their pet. They can then write it their own way or it could be scribed for them by an adult or an older peer tutor. Older students (six to eight years) might be asked to list the things they loved about their pet, some funny habits and why they gave it the name it has(had).

All of these pictures and comments could then be compiled to form a book titled *Our Special Pets*. This book should be made available for students to borrow. Some might even like to take it home to share with parents.

### LESSON 2

This lesson would follow a couple of days after the first reading and would aim to look more closely at the theme of death.

**Procedure**

Read the story for the second time.

Remind the class of the discussion about the story last time and their *Our Special Pets* book. Read and show several entries from the class book.

Ask if class members can ever remember one of their special pets dying. **Note** If some had mentioned this in the previous lesson simply refer to their comments. How did the pet die? How did they feel when their pet died?

Write down some of the class members' feelings on the board. Ask them if they ended up getting another pet, or whether, like Elfie's owner they decided not to. Why did they decide this?

**Follow-up activities**

As a follow-up to the above lesson either on the same day or in some other lesson turn the list of feelings into a class poem titled 'The Day My Pet Died'. List all their feelings after an initial first line which might be: 'The day my pet died I felt...' You might end the poem with the line 'But I'll always love it'.

### The Day My Pet Died
by 2 Yellow

The day my pet died I felt...
Sad,
Sick,
Lonely,
Like running away,
Really angry,
All alone,
Upset,
Like hiding from everyone,
Like crying,
Really really cranky,
But I'll always love it.

## LESSON 3

The aim of this lesson is to introduce *Granpa* (Burningham 1980) and to look at the nature of the relationships we share with people we love. How do we spend time with them? What do we expect of each other?

It is necessary to point out that the way this book is dealt with will vary depending upon the age of your class and the way in which they respond to the death of Granpa. Some young children will fail to see that Granpa has died. If that happens then you will need to decide whether it is necessary to deal with death at all with this book. However, within the context of this program it would be desirable, and relatively painless to deal with this theme. However, preferably it should not be dealt with in the first lesson (see lesson 4).

## Procedure

Read *Granpa* to the class without comment.

After the reading ask your class whether they liked this book. Why or why not? If some children comment on the disjointed nature of the text it might be necessary to point out that Burningham has done this because it is the way conversations between an adult and a young child often take place. You might then need to re-read parts, or all of the book.

By Louise (age 9)

Macdonalds

Macdonalds now has breakfa

Poppy taking me to Macdonalds

*Example of one child's sketch in response to the invitation to draw themselves spending time with Grandpa doing their 'favourite thing'.*

Following the initial discussion, ask your students if they spend a lot of time with a grandma or grandpa (you might discuss all the names they use for their grandparents). If some children don't have grandparents you might ask them if there is another adult with whom they spend lots of time, e.g. a parent, aunt, friend of the family. Ask them to share the way they spend their time together. What things do they find most special? Record all of these ideas on the board or on overhead.

### Follow-up activities

a) As an extension to this lesson have older children complete a list of the favourite things they do with their adult companion. Perhaps title the list 'Things I Like Doing With...'. They might also like to draw a picture of doing the thing they like most. Younger children might simply draw the picture and dictate a caption. These pictures could be used to make a wall frieze.

b) Written conversation between Granpa and the little girl.

## LESSON 4

The primary purpose is to allow the class to discuss the theme of death, relating it to their own lives and experiences.

**Note** This lesson requires considerable sensitivity. Be sensitive to the fact that some children may have lost people close to them quite recently.

### Procedure

Re-read *Granpa* to the class.

At the end of the reading show the class the picture of the empty chair and ask them why John Burningham drew it. What does it mean? If someone had already commented on this in a previous lesson simply refer to these comments.

Allow all children to express their opinions then indicate that one common interpretation is that the author wanted to show that Granpa had died. Ask the class to think about other parts of the story that might have given a clue that Granpa was going to die. Look at each of these pages and discuss them.

After a full discussion of the book ask the class whether they have ever had someone close to them die. Ask them if they are able to share who it was, what happened to them and how they felt at the time. What do they miss most about this person?

Finish the lesson by looking at the last page and asking the class to indicate why John Burningham might have drawn this picture. What was he trying to say? Accept all responses but make sure the class has time to discuss the commonly held view that this page means 'life goes on'. Talk about this viewpoint and its significance for those who lose loved ones.

**LESSON 5**

The major purpose is to introduce *John Brown, Rose, and the Midnight Cat* (Wagner 1977) and to look once again at the theme of caring for, and sharing your life with someone you love.

**Procedure**

Read *John Brown, Rose, and the Midnight Cat* without comment.

Following the reading allow time for general responses to the story then ask the class to consider the question: Why didn't John Brown want to let the Midnight Cat in?

Break the class into groups of three or four (whether you do this with younger groups will depend upon how self-directed they can be), and ask them to brainstorm all the reasons John Brown gave (and might have given) for not allowing the Midnight Cat to come inside. Select a group leader to record the group's responses. Come back together as a class to discuss the ideas.

If you wish to keep a record of the ideas shared create a wallchart titled 'Why We Don't Need a Black Cat...' by John Brown.

### Why We Don't Need a Black Cat...

We don't need a cat because...
You've got me,
It will just sleep on the lounge,
It will drink all the milk,
Cats make me nervous,
Cats are sneaky,
Dogs are supposed to be man's best friend,
I'll leave home if you let it in.

by John Brown

**Follow-up activities**

As an extension to this lesson you might select students in pairs to dramatise a conversation in which John Brown tries to convince Rose that they don't need a cat.

You might also extend the lesson by asking your students to think about times when they felt jealous of another person who threatened to come between them and a friend. How did they feel? What did they do about it? Provide an opportunity for selected students to role-play one of these situations in the form of a moral dilemma story. The class should observe the dramatisation and be asked to comment upon the action that the characters should take.

**LESSON 6**

The focus in this lesson will vary depending on whether you deal with Wagner's use of the Midnight Cat to represent death ( a fairly abstract interpretation for young children). If you don't then the lesson will be concerned with the way in which John Brown relents and lets the cat in. Why does he do it?

If dealing with the theme of death it is important to allow the class to simply enjoy the story at their own level first and to present the death theme as only one interpretation, not *the* interpretation. An attempt would also be made to link the book with the previous picture books in this program.

### Procedure

Re-read the story without comment.

Ask the class why they think John Brown finally gave in and let the cat inside. You might need to introduce the idea that relationships often involve 'give and take'. How big a concession did John Brown make?

After a full discussion of this dimension of relationships, introduce the idea that Wagner used the Midnight Cat to represent death, and that some readers like this interpretation. Explain how and why she attempts to do this. Discuss the consequences of the fact that John Brown 'lets the cat in'. Re-read the book once more and provide time for the class to respond again.

Finish the lesson by pointing out that all three books read (in this program) have dealt with death. Ask them which one they feel did it the best. Why?

### Follow-up activities

If you wish to pursue the theme of death in children's books (I'd wait for perhaps a month or two), you might consider reading *Charlotte's Web* (White 1952) to the class.

## LESSON 7

The purpose of this lesson is to re-examine the theme of love and draw together the way in which each of the authors have provided insights into different expressions of love.

### Procedure

Begin by reminding (and showing) the class the three books that have been shared. Point out that each of these stories deals with the relationship between two characters who love each other very deeply. Ask the class to indicate the identity of the characters. Write them on the board. Suggest to your students that they think of all the ways the characters showed their love for each other. Provide a simple stencilled sheet (see the example below) with appropriate headings and break the class into groups of three to five to share ideas.

**Note** With younger children this would be done together as a class with the teacher recording responses on the board or on overhead.

## Caring and Sharing

| Character | How they showed their love |
|---|---|
| Elfie's master | |
| Elfie | |
| Granpa | |
| The little girl | |
| John Brown | |
| Rose | |

When the groups have completed their sheets, have them share some of the answers with the class.

### Follow-up activities

As a follow-up to the above activity you might suggest that your students write a 'Love is...' poem. Younger children would complete this with the teacher, while older children could complete their own or do one with a partner.

Suggest to the class that they use ideas from the previous activity to write their poem.

### Love is...

Love is...
Worrying about the people you love,
Sharing things with others,
Spending time with someone special,
Always showing someone you care,
Making mud pies together,
Looking after someone,
Not wanting to let someone go.

Share the poems that are written and display them so that others can read them.

CHAPTER EIGHT  # I Remember When

**Literature:** *Penny Pollard's Diary*, Robin Klein
*Wilfrid Gordon McDonald Partridge*, Mem Fox
**Suggested Level:** Grades one to three

## SYNOPSES

*Penny Pollard's Diary* (1987)
As the title implies, this book is a diary. It is the diary of a rather unusual girl about ten years of age named Penny Pollard. Penny is forever at odds with the people around her. When her mother wants her to look pretty, she wants to wear jeans and 'spike' her hair. When her teacher wants her to join the class to entertain elderly people at a home, she rebels because she claims that 'old people (are) just plain boring' (p. 5).

However, Penny is forced to go to the old people's home in spite of her best efforts to avoid it. Not to be outdone, Penny slips out of the room during a choir item to sit in the garden and eat some cake she steals from the afternoon tea table. Little does Penny know that she will meet an old lady (Mrs Bettany) with just as much spirit and cunning as she. A bond of friendship develops between the two of them as Penny discovers Mrs B. (as she comes to call her) understands her better than anyone she knows.

*Wilfrid Gordon McDonald Partridge* (1985)
Wilfrid is a small boy with a big name who lives next to an old people's home. He spends a lot of time visiting people in the home, but likes most of all to spend time with Miss Nancy Alison Delacourt Cooper, because she too has a long name. One day Wilfrid learns that Miss Nancy has 'lost' her memory, so it is not surprising that he sets off to find it for her.

## PROGRAM FOCUS

The major emphases within this program are:
a) An examination of the special relationship that can exist between a child and an elderly person. What does each of these books teach us about old age? About the needs of old people? What are the special problems that old people face when coping with their worlds?

b) The exploration of the theme of memories. What's a memory? What things stimulate our memories? How do memories vary? What is the relationship between memories and the objects of our world?

## POSSIBLE LESSONS

### LESSON 1

The major focus is the central character of Penny Pollard. What is she like? Why is she the type of person she is? Is she like any real people the students know?

### Procedure

Introduce *Penny Pollard's Diary* to the class and comment briefly upon the form this unusual 'story' takes. Explain that it isn't really a story (i.e. a piece of prose), but that it does 'tell a story'.

Read the first three days in Penny's diary (pp.4-9).

Ask the class to comment on Penny. What is she like? Is she like anyone you know? Break the class up into groups of four to six to answer the question 'What is Penny like?' Brainstorm Penny's characteristics. After five or ten minutes have the groups come together to share their ideas.

Name: Simone
Alias: Prissy
Age: 10
Address: 13 Primrose St
Description: A very babyish kind of girl - very girlish who plays with barbie dolls
Special Features: blonde hair, dimples, smells nice blue eyes very clean
Major Goals in Life: To be just a housewife with lots of kids
Unusual or Interesting Habits. Plays with barbie dolls

Nikki (age 12 yrs)

*Nikki's mugsheet on Simone from the book 'Penny Pollard's Diary'*

Invite the students to prepare a character mugsheet (see Cairney 1985a) for either Penny or Simone. Encourage them to think about the personalities of their character as they complete the details of the mugsheet.

**Follow-up activities**

Some pupils might like to draw a picture of Penny to show what they think she looks like. Make up a wall display using all the drawings.

### LESSON 2

The major purpose of this lesson is to look more closely at the growing relationship between Mrs Bettany and Penny. Of particular interest is the way in which Penny's growing knowledge of Mrs Bettany leads to a greater appreciation of her as a person. Penny realises that Mrs Bettany is a person of great worth.

**Procedure**

Read pp. 10-12 of Monday's entry, stopping at the point when Penny says:

> Felt very depressed looking at the old people. They looked like flowers fading at the end of summer, or echoes. All wearing tired faded whispery colours — pale grey, wishy-washy blue, mauve.

Ask the class what Penny means by 'flowers fading' and 'echoes'. What does this show about her feelings towards old people? Ask the class if they feel the same way about old people. Why might Penny have felt like this?

Read the rest of Monday's entry (pp. 12-21). What does Penny learn about Mrs Bettany? As a class ask the students to list the things Penny learnt about Mrs Bettany that surprised her. How did these things start to change her views of at least this one old person? Why do they get on so well?

### LESSON 3

The major purpose of this lesson is to discuss the importance of memories for all people. What do memories permit us to do as people? The lesson will also touch on the sensitive theme that emerges in this book concerning the slow removal of freedom from old people, as well as the tendency for old people to slowly become dispossessed of their earlier lives.

**Procedure**

Read Tuesday's entry (pp. 22-3) of Penny's diary. What was the significance of Mrs Bettany being the first person to look at her swap cards properly? What did this show?

Ask the students whether they collect things. Ask them to tell the class about these collections. Do they share them with other people? Which people take the most interest in them?

Read Wednesday's entry (pp. 24-31). At the end of the reading break the class into groups of three to five to brainstorm the memories that Mrs Bettany shared with Penny.

As a class have the students share their memories so that a comprehensive list can be made on the board. How does Penny react to Mrs Bettany's reminiscences? Why is the memory of her house so important to her?

**Note** It is important here to ensure that the students consider the fact that Mrs Bettany's memory could have been particularly important because as an old person all the concrete signs of her earlier life had gone. All that remains are her memories. Robin Klein has indicated that the experience of not having any 'thing' from her childhood makes her very sad.

### Follow-up activities

As a follow-up to this lesson you might consider arranging a visit to an old people's home so that the students can interview elderly residents. Using a prepared interview schedule (which can be devised with the class), and working in pairs, they might ask elderly people to share some of their childhood memories.

#### *Sample Survey of Childhood Memories*

Hi, we'd like to ask you a few questions about your childhood. We want to find out how your life was different to our lives today.

1. When you were young did you go to school?
2. What was school like?
3. What was your home like?
4. What did you do in your spare time?
5. Can you remember special games you played?
6. What is the saddest memory you have of your childhood?
7. What is the best memory you have of your childhood?
8. Is there anything else that you can remember that you'd like to tell us?

Thanks very much for talking with us, we've learnt a lot about you.

### LESSON 4

The purpose of this lesson is to explore memories and the role objects play in stimulating memories. To do this another book will be used — *Wilfrid Gordon McDonald Partridge* (Fox 1985). The aim is also to encourage students to see how in the same way that memories were important to Mrs Bettany (in *Penny Pollard's Diary*) and Miss Nancy (in *Wilfrid Gordon McDonald Partridge*), so too they are important for children.

### Procedure

Read the story right through without comment. After the reading direct the class to the section of the story where Wilfrid decides to find out about memories after overhearing his parents saying that Miss Nancy had lost hers. Ask the class to recall all the things mentioned by his friends which represent memories. List them on the board. After this ask them to recall the things which Wilfrid collects for Miss Nancy.

### Special Things for Miss Nancy

a box of shells
a puppet on a string
his grandfather's medal
his precious football
a fresh, warm egg

Ask the class to try to think of things in their own lives that bring back memories. Break the class into groups of two to four to discuss 'Memories'. **Note** Whether you do this with younger children depends on the degree of independence that they have developed.

Bring the class back together to share the memories. List them on the board under the heading 'Memories' and with the first line 'I remember when...'

### Memories

I remember when...
My little brother was born,
Dad got a new job,
My dog Cybil died,
Uncle Eric had a car accident,
I was in Kindergarten,
I won the cross-country race last year,
Mrs Stokes was our teacher in Kinder,
We went to Scotland for a holiday,
My Dad left home.

### Follow-up activities

Some students might like to draw their own special memories. Use these drawings to create a display of class memories.

### LESSON 5

The major purpose is to build on the previous lesson and examine in more detail the links that exist between objects and memories.

### Procedure

Read Saturday's entry in Penny's diary (pp. 32-9).

After reading discuss the trip to see Mrs Bettany's house. Discuss the disappointment that Mrs Bettany must have experienced. What would it have meant to see that her house had been demolished? Why was it so special that she found a piece of her geranium still growing?

Re-read the dialogue between Mrs Bettany and Penny as they walk nearer and nearer to her old homesite (pp. 34-6). Provide a typed copy of the dialogue in this section of the text (place the narration in brackets or parentheses) and ask the students to dramatise this conversation in pairs. After approximately five to ten minutes ask some of these pairs to present their dramatisations to the class.

**Follow-up activities**

As a follow-up you might share the Nadia Wheatley and Donna Rawlins book *My Place* (Wheatley & Rawlins, 1987). Of particular interest is the fact that *My Place* shows so clearly how places change in time. Things are demolished, new things are built, but often if you look carefully, remnants of earlier times (and people) remain. Discuss the fact that memories and things are so closely tied.

## LESSON 6

The purpose of this lesson is to focus more closely on the growing relationship between Penny and Mrs Bettany. As well, the lesson would consider the importance of gifts. Why do we give gifts? What makes a gift special? Is it just the price?

### Procedure

Read Sunday's entry from Penny's diary (pp. 40-1).

Discuss Penny's gift to Mrs Bettany. Why was it such a special gift? Ask your students to share the details of any special gift they have received with which they were pleased, not simply because it was something expensive, or something they needed. Ask them to talk about these gifts in small groups of two to four. Why were they so special?

Read Monday's entry from Penny's diary (pp. 42-7).

Ask your students to once again brainstorm a list of the things Mrs Bettany remembers. Why were they so special? Why is it that she keeps talking about her husband Albert as if he is still alive? What does this show?

## LESSON 7

The major purpose is to encourage students to reflect upon the things that Penny has learned about old people as a result of her experiences with Mrs Bettany. The lesson is also designed to encourage students to reflect upon their own attitudes towards old people. This should provide a good culmination to the whole program.

### Procedure

Read Tuesday's entry from Penny's diary (pp. 48-51).

Following the reading allow time for all students to respond in general terms to the book. Did they like it? Why or why not? What did they think of the two main characters? Would they like them in real life?

After this initial discussion ask your students to reflect upon the things Penny learnt about Mrs Bettany from spending so much time with her. What did she learn about old people in general? Do you think her opinion of old people would have changed? If so, in what ways?

Finish the lesson by discussing the special nature of the relationship between Mrs Bettany and Penny, and Wilfrid and Miss Nancy. Why did they have such good relationships? What made them such good friends? What was special about the way each person treated the other?

CHAPTER NINE # Today Was a Terrible Day

**Literature:** *Today Was a Terrible Day* (1980), Patricia Reilly Giff
*Alexander and the Terrible, Horrible, No Good, Very Bad Day*
(1987), Judith Viorst

**Suggested Level:** Grade two

## SYNOPSES

*Today Was a Terrible Day* (1980)
This is the story of a particularly bad day in the life of Ronald Morgan. The story chronicles a series of disastrous events that start from the moment Ronald arrives at school on the ill fated day. It is an amusing account of everyday situations and predicaments with which few children would have difficulty identifying.

*Alexander and the Terrible, Horrible, No Good, Very Bad Day* (1987)
Viorst, like Giff has attempted to show the funny side of everyday lifetime problems. Like Ronald Morgan, Anthony battles everyday problems. From the moment he rises from bed Anthony knows that it is going to be a 'terrible, horrible, no good, very bad day.'

## PROGRAM FOCUS

The major purpose of this program is to examine the theme 'life wasn't meant to be easy'. Both books provide an insight into the problems of life. In the mundane events of the day there always seems to be unlimited potential for chaos. And yet, life is all about learning to cope with adversity. The two major characters in the books chosen learn this lesson the hard way.

As these books are examined students will be encouraged to:
a) Relate the events of each story to their lives.
b) Reflect upon the events that occur.
c) Examine the way each author uses everyday events to amuse the reader.

━━━━━━━━ POSSIBLE LESSONS

### LESSON 1

The major purposes of this lesson are to introduce *Alexander and the Terrible, Horrible, No Good, Very Bad Day*, engage the students with the story and encourage them to relate Alexander's experiences to their own.

#### Procedure

Before reading the book, display the cover and read the title and author's name. Ask the class to predict what this story might be about. What might be the reason for Alexander's 'terrible, horrible, no good, very bad day'?

Read the first page of the story and ask the class if they have ever had days when they knew as soon as they got up that things were going to go wrong? Break the class into groups of four to six students and have them share their experiences.

Read the rest of the book and provide time for students to respond in general terms. What did they think of the story? Did it remind them of experiences they have had?

#### Follow-up activities

After the lesson some students might like to draw an incident from one of their own terrible days.

### LESSON 2

The purpose of this lesson is to provide an opportunity for students to explore one of the major themes that readers recognize when they encounter this book - 'life wasn't meant to be easy.'

#### Procedure

Introduce the book once more and indicate to the class that you intend reading it again to look more closely at all the problems Alexander experiences. Read the book right through without interruption.

Break the class up into groups and ask them to recall and list all the bad things that happened to Alexander and create a picture story sequence showing the details.

Display the picture story sequences and discuss the events and their impact on Alexander. Ask the class to consider how difficult it would be to cope with all the problems Alexander encountered.

#### Follow-up activities

As a follow-up to this lesson invite your students to select one incident from the story for dramatisation. Break the class into groups of three to five students and allow time for students to rehearse. Later, provide an opportunity for some students to present their performance to the class.

Alternatively, you might simply provide an extract of one incident for students and provide an opportunity for them to rehearse and present a dramatic reading of it.

*The End of a Terrible, Horrible, No Good, Very Bad Day*

## LESSON 3

This lesson is designed to provide students with an additional opportunity to reflect upon the previously identified theme - 'life wasn't meant to be easy.'

### Procedure

Begin by referring to the previous lesson and the discussion concerning Alexander's problems. Re-read the first few pages in which Alexander suggests he might move to Australia. Break the class into groups of three to four and ask them to discuss why he constantly talks about moving to Australia. Why would he choose Australia?

When the groups have discussed these questions encourage them to share their ideas with the whole class. Point out to the class that a version of this book is published in Australia for Australian children and refers instead to Timbuktu. Show the class a map of the world and locate the USA, Australia and Timbuktu. Why are the locations of these places so important? Ask the class to think about the things they do when life gets tough.

Brainstorm problems that the children commonly have and possible responses to each. Write them on the board and discuss them as a class.

### *Sample responses from one group invited to think of ways out of predicaments*

| Predicament | Response |
| --- | --- |
| Being late for class | Sneak in the back way |
| Turning to tell your friend not to talk just as the teacher looks | Pretend you were just yawning |
| Forgetting your homework | Ask to go to the bathroom just before it's marked |
| Leaving your sweater at school for the third day in a row | Go without one the next day and hope your mom doesn't notice. |

### Follow-up activities

As a follow-up to this lesson you might try to obtain the video *Alexander and the Terrible, Horrible, No Good, Very Bad Day* (Haak 1989). This fourteen minute colour video uses live actors and is a reasonably faithful reproduction of the story.

## LESSON 4

The aim of this lesson is to introduce *Today Was a Terrible Day* encouraging the class to engage with the story line and relate the events to their lives and experiences.

### Procedure

Introduce the book by showing the cover and sharing the title. If anyone makes links between this book and Viorst's story allow time to discuss the reasons for making such a link.

Read the book without making any comments, but stop at the point where Ronald opens the note from his teacher on the way home. Before you read the version of the note from the book ask the students to predict what might be in it.

After allowing time for general class discussion and response invite students to write their own versions of the note.

Read the rest of the story. After the reading, break the class into groups of three to five students to discuss the outcome of the story and the accuracy of their predictions about the note. Provide time for them to compare their ideas and a brief time for the whole class to share its predictions.

January 16th

Dear Ronald,

Today has been a terrible day. I find it hard to believe that one person could cause so much trouble.

Might I suggest a good nights sleep. I hope tomorrow you return as a <u>new person</u>.

Yours Faithfully,
Miss Tyler

P.S. You might also consider how you will replace the broken pot.

*One student's predicted note from Miss Tyler to Ronald Morgan*

71

**LESSON 5**

The major aim of this lesson is to help the class to empathise with Ronald Morgan and reflect upon the essential features of his character.

**Procedure**

Re-read the book without interruption. At the conclusion of the story allow time for responses of a general nature, then ask the class to more closely discuss the parallels between the problems of Ronald Morgan and Alexander. Ask your students to comment upon the way each of the characters deals with the problems. Encourage them to compare the way these two story characters deal with problems, compared with their own real=life efforts to deal with problems.

After the discussion invite the class to create a book titled - *Today Was a Terrible Day*. Ask the students to find a partner and discuss some of the terrible things that happen when they have a bad day. Suggest that they compile a list of these incidents.

Ask specific students to share their incidents and then demonstrate how these ideas can be turned into a poem using a standard first and last line.

*A poem composed from a list of incidents*
*that occurred on a 'terrible day'*

> Today was a terrible day...
> Frank ate all the Cornflakes,
> Both my shoelaces broke,
> Mrs Slack's dog chased me for seven blocks,
> I forgot my homework,
> Ms Casey was away and we had grumpy Gresford,
> We had to do 35 math problems,
> Mom was late home from work,
> My favourite TV show wasn't on,
> We had meatballs for supper,
> I guess some days are like that.

**Follow-up activities**

Some students might want to focus more upon the central character of Ronald Morgan (alias Snakey) by creating a police 'Wanted' poster for him. These could include a picture, description, major crimes committed by characters, unusual habits, last known whereabouts, finger prints, etc.

**LESSON 6**

The major purpose of this lesson is to once again help students empathise with the main characters in each of the books, and encourage them to relate the lessons learned to their own lives.

**Procedure**

Break the class into groups of four to six students and preferably provide a copy of each book for students to re-read or peruse. Encourage them to reflect upon the troubles that each character experienced in the stories and to discuss the way each dealt with them.

Suggest that each student attempt to write a diary entry for either character that might have been written at the end of the 'terrible day'. If you have a less able class this can be completed as a group with the text being jointly constructed.

Finally, provide time for these diary entries to be read to the group and discussed. One student wrote the following entry.

*Monday October 5th*

*Well today started out like one of those days where you wish you were dead. Every time I turned around I got into trouble. Everyone called me 'Snakey', I got caught eating, Rosemary was a real _____, I lost my money, AND worst of all, broke one of our plant pots! Then Miss Tyler gave me a note to take home and I thought I was dead. But the good news was Miss Tyler just wanted to cheer me up. I think she's great. I can't imagine Mrs Jones doing something like that. Boy do I hope that I miss out on her next year.*

*Ronald*

One student's diary entry for 'Today was a Terrible Day.'

### Follow-up activities

Suggest that the class complete character rating scales for Ronald Morgan and Alexander. Rating scales are a simple way to comment upon the personality traits of characters. Provide a series of personality traits (the students can choose some of their own) and suggest that each character is rated. For example, one student used the following traits to assess the main characters in these stories:

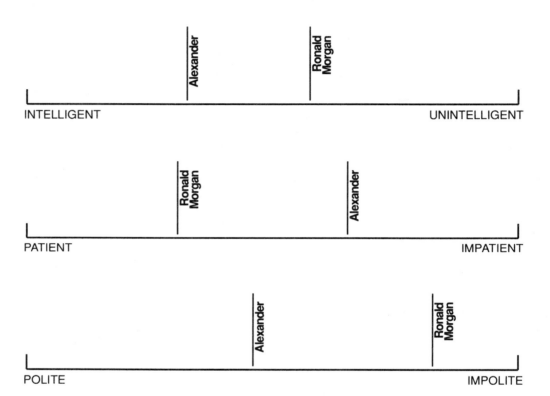

| INTELLIGENT | | UNINTELLIGENT |
| PATIENT | | IMPATIENT |
| POLITE | | IMPOLITE |

When everyone has had an opportunity to rate the characters using the traits selected, provide an opportunity for all students to share their ratings. Ask students who present alternative points of view to justify their decisions.

### LESSON 7

The purpose of this final lesson is simply to provide an opportunity for students to look for links between each of the two books they have been reading. This lesson could occur as a culmination to Lesson 6 or could be dealt with on a different day.

### Procedure

As in Lesson 6 it is desirable to have multiple copies of both books available if possible. If insufficient copies are available this lesson can be given by completing it with one small group at a time.

Break the class into groups of four to six students, provide a copy of both books and ask them to spend time discussing each. Provide some general questions to stimulate their discussion. For example:

- Did you like both books? Why or why not?
- How were they similar and different? List these in point form.
- Were there particular incidents to which you could easily relate? If so, share these with the group.

Encourage the group to be prepared to ask their own questions if their discussion moves beyond these issues. Suggest also that the groups share the details of other books which seem related to the books read, and to offer an explanation of the links they see between each of them.

Finally, when all groups have completed their discussions provide time for each to share its insights with the whole class.

CHAPTER TEN

# Farmer Schulz's Ducks

**Literature:** *Farmer Schulz's Ducks* (1988), Colin Thiele
**Suggested Level:** Grades two to three

## SYNOPSIS

Farmer Schulz just loves his ducks and gives them the freedom of the countryside at his farm on the Onkaparinga River. Each day the ducks walk nonchalantly across the road and down to the river to swim. However, problems start for Farmer Schulz as the traffic flow along the road increases, and motorists stop worrying about the safety of the ducks. Farmer Schulz and his family try many solutions to the problems that arise, but have limited success until one day Anna, the youngest of the Schulz children, comes up with a perfect solution.

## PROGRAM FOCUS

While there are many teaching points that arise from this picture book, the major emphases in this program will be:
a) The setting that Thiele has chosen for the story.
b) Thiele's ability to describe settings and people with lively detail.
c) The use made of language by the author to communicate the rich Anglo/German dialect.
d) The impact that environmental changes have on people, places and animals.

## POSSIBLE LESSONS

### LESSON 1
The major focus is the setting that Thiele has selected for his story. Encourage the class to imagine the valley, the house, and the farmyard, so that they have a full appreciation of the beautiful setting that Thiele selects for the story.

## Procedure

Begin the reading of the novel, stopping at the point where the valley becomes busier and the motorists less and less patient, until finally it reaches the point where: 'Sometimes they didn't even stop for the ducks!'

Ask the class for their reactions to the description of the Onkaparinga River. How does Colin Thiele's description make you feel? Have you ever been to a place as beautiful as this? Ask the class to close their eyes while you read the first three pages again. Ask them to try to picture it in their minds.

As a class prepare a wall frieze or collage of the river, the valley, and the ducks.

*Sample picture of Schulz's cellar*

### Follow-up activities

As a follow-up to the above read the description of Farmer Schulz's house and farmyard. Ask your students to either: draw the house, draw the cellar, or prepare a map of the valley and the farmyard.

An additional activity would be to read Thiele's description of the Coorong in *Storm Boy* (1987). Ask them to comment on Thiele's mastery of description.

### LESSON 2

The purpose is to engage the class more fully by encouraging them to predict the story plot. Sketch to stretch will be used to enable the students to represent their predictions.

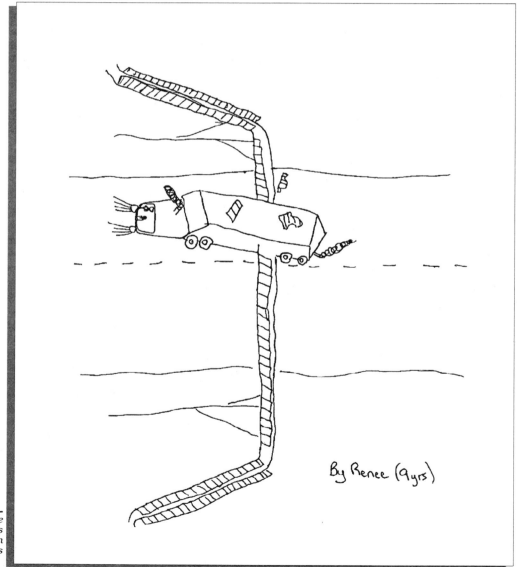

*Renee's sketch of 'the disaster' that was about to occur in 'Farmer Schulz's Ducks'*

**Procedure**

Continue reading the story, stopping after Farmer Schulz has constructed the bridge, at the point where the reader is told, 'But a great disaster was coming, and it arrived on the first of March.'

Encourage the class to predict what the disaster might be, using sketch to stretch to represent their ideas. When they have finished their sketches break the class into groups of two to four to share their predictions.

**Follow-up activities**

Re-read the section of the story where the family discusses suitable signs to be placed by the road to warn motorists. Suggest to the class that they should create their own signs using either their own slogans or those of the family. Display the signs around the room.

## LESSON 3

The purpose is to focus on Farmer Schulz as a character. One of the simplest ways to help readers relate to a character is through dramatisation. A secondary interest in this lesson will be the way in which Thiele uses invented language to provide the reader with Farmer Schulz's special Anglo/German dialect.

**Procedure**

Re-read the section of the story where Farmer Schulz becomes angry at the death and injury to his ducks caused by the driver overtaking a truck. Start where the reader is told Farmer Schulz's face was the colour of one of his ducks — '...mottled and blue and purple...' End at the point where Farmer Schulz says 'Dey vill all go over d'top.'

Provide typed copies of this piece of dialogue between Farmer Schulz and his family and ask your students to dramatise it in groups of three. When they have had sufficient time ask some groups to present their dramatisation to the whole class.

After presenting the dramatisations ask the class to look more closely at the way Thiele has used invented spelling to create Farmer Schulz's dialect.

**Follow-up activities**

Refer to the discussion of Farmer Schulz's language in the last lesson. Invite students to create some original dialogue between Farmer Schulz and his family using invented spelling to convey the richness of the dialect (see the example below).

### *The Great Duck Sale*

'Schildren, I haf desided to sell da ducks,' announced Farmer Schulz.

'What!' exclaimed Hans. 'Father, you know you could never sell the ducks.'

'But vot is de use,' cried Farmer Schulz. 'First, I cannot dis killing off my ducks to schtop. Den, vwhen I did dis killing schtop, I hav to put up with de tourists who my ducks dey all the time must come to vatch.'

'Oh father, we can find a way to stop that. Leave it to Anna and me, we can find a solution. Right Anna?' said Hans.

'Oh you schildren, are schmarter dan Einstein.'

If your students find this lesson stimulating and enjoyable you might ask them to dramatise the earlier passage where the family debates the type of sign needed on the side of the road to warn motorists.

## LESSON 4

The major purpose is to complete the story and encourage the class to evaluate the solution to Farmer Schulz's problem. Was it satisfactory? Could there be future problems? Were there other solutions?

### Procedure

Complete the reading of the story. After the reading allow time for general responses, then ask students to comment on Anna's solution to the problem. Was it a good solution? Could she have solved the problem another way? Could there be problems with a duck pipe? What could happen?

Break the class up into groups of three to five to discuss other solutions to the problem. Suggest that the group record all suggestions and that they choose one to develop more fully.

Ask them to prepare drawings or plans to accompany their idea. Provide time for all groups to share their ideas then display them around the room.

Hold a brief discussion concerning the problems Farmer Schulz experienced trying to get approval for the 'duck pipe'. Why were the procedures so complicated? Would it be as difficult if we wanted to construct a duck pipe?

### Follow-up activities

a) Write a letter to your local council explaining that the class has been reading a story in which a farmer tries to have a pipe placed under a road to allow ducks to cross in safety. Ask the town clerk to provide information (hypothetically) on the procedures that would need to be followed if the class wanted to do the same thing. Make it clear to the council that you have no intention of doing this, but would be interested to know how difficult it might be.

b) Dramatise the meeting between Farmer Schulz and the government and council officials.

## LESSON 5

The purpose of this lesson is to allow the class to reflect upon the whole story, discuss the major details of the plot, and respond in writing by preparing a newspaper account of Farmer Schulz's problems.

### Procedure

Re-read the story without interruption. After the story, ask the class to consider how a newspaper might write an article about Farmer Schulz and his ducks. Show an example of a human interest article and discuss its features. Look particularly at the fact that articles typically answer the questions: Who? What? When? Where? Why?

Break the class into groups of two to four to prepare an article which:

- **Describes** Farmer Schulz and his family, his ducks, the farm and the Onkaparinga River.
- **Tells** the reader about his problems with increasing traffic.
- **Recounts** Farmer Schulz's failed attempt to solve the problem with a bridge.
- **Describes** the final solution to his problem.
- **Comments** on Farmer Schulz, his farm and the ducks.

## LESSON 6

The purpose of this lesson is to consider the impact that environmental changes have on people, places and our native flora and fauna. How evident is this theme in the book?

### Procedure

Ask the class to reflect upon the story and to list all the ways the Onkaparinga River valley changed. Brainstorm changes as a class and list them on the board or on overhead. When these have been listed brainstorm the consequences of each change. Finally, attempt to arrive at solutions to these problems. It might be useful to place the outcomes of this lesson in table form (see the example below).

### Changes to the Onkaparinga River Valley

| Changes | Problems | Solutions |
|---------|----------|-----------|
| More people | This meant more cars. | Advertise the use of car pools; start a bus service. |
| The city spread | More people needed to live close to Farmer Schulz. | Build more flats in the city. |
| More houses | This meant that the roads became more congested. | Build better roads away from the river and the farms. |
| More cars | This meant that people took longer to get to work and became impatient. | Advertise the dangers of impatient drivers and the benefits of buses and car sharing. |

Share details of real life examples of the way in which changes in traffic conditions can have a big impact upon people, flora and fauna.

For example, the death of Australian native animals like koalas, kangaroos, wombats and many species of birds hit by vehicles on major highways which split their natural territories in two. It may be possible to collect newspaper clippings of interest.

In rural locations it may also be possible to survey a strip of highway recording observations of any wildlife found injured or killed. It would also be useful to record observations of any other signs of humans' impact on the environment.

**Follow-up activities**

a) Some students might like to conduct research work on the impact of highways on a specific species of animal. An outcome of this research work might be to prepare a poster warning the public about the consequences that the intrusion of traffic can have on the environment.

b) Share other books that deal with the theme of humans' impact upon the world. For example: *Where the Forest Meets the Sea* (1988) by Jeannie Baker, *My Place* (1987) by Nadia Wheatley and Donna Rawlins. How do the authors of these books deal with this theme? Are there similarities?

CHAPTER ELEVEN

# Fantastic Mr Fox

**Literature:** *Fantastic Mr Fox* (1988), Roald Dahl
**Suggested Level:** Grades two to three

## SYNOPSIS

This is the story of a den of cunning foxes and their ongoing battle to outsmart a repulsive group of farmers by the names of Boggis, Bunce and Bean. For years Mr Fox has been stealing from the farmers by using cunning, bravery and a secret weapon — a complex network of tunnels beneath the properties. However, Boggis, Bunce and Bean finally decide enough is enough and set about the task of destroying Mr Fox and his family in a frenzy of digging, shooting and cursing.

## PROGRAM FOCUS

While there are many features of interest, the following would be of primary importance in this program:
a) Dahl's development of characters and his ability to create believable relationships between them.
b) The setting for the story.
c) The emotions and feelings of the characters in response to the events of the conflict.

## POSSIBLE LESSONS

### LESSON 1

The major focus will be the key characters and the setting. The lesson will include discussion of each of the characters, as well as the valley where the story is set.

**Procedure**

Read chapters 1 and 2, showing the illustrations.

Allow time for general responses to the story. What do you think of Mr Fox? What about Boggis, Bunce and Bean? What are they going to do?

*A map of Mr Fox's world based on the book 'Fantastic Mr Fox'*

After the initial discussion suggest to your students that they draw a picture of the valley showing where the Fox family and the farmers live. Suggest that this could simply be a picture, or a pictorial map.

Suggest to the class that they create a character mugsheet (see Cairney 1985a) for one of the main characters. Stress to them that some of the details need to be invented, but that they need to be consistent with the character and plot of the story.

### Follow-up activities

Suggest to the class that they begin a diary for one of the characters in the story (Mr and Mrs Fox and their children, Boggis, Bunce, and Bean). Show them a diary and read several entries from it (*Penny Pollard's Diary* (Klein 1987) is an ideal example to use), stressing the form that it takes, the personal nature of the writing etc. Provide a small book within which to keep the diary entry (e.g. an exercise book cut in two) and stress that they will need to write in it after each section of the story is read.

### LESSON 2

The major purpose is to focus on the thoughts and motives of the farmers and their perceptions of the various characters. How would each view the situation differently? Who would feel most in control of the situation?

### Procedure

Commence reading chapter 3 and stop at the point where the farmers fire their guns — 'Bang-bang! Bang-bang! Bang-bang!'. Ask the students to use sketch to stretch to show what has happened.

to share these sketches in groups of four to six students. Ask all students to explain their sketches and provide reasons for their predictions.

After the sketches have been discussed complete the chapter. Ask them to consider whether their predictions were correct.

Read chapter 4. Ask the students to consider how the Foxes would be feeling as the noise of the shovels scrape and scratch above them. How might the children feel? What would be their greatest fears?

### Follow-up activities

Continue the diaries begun in the first lesson. Encourage the students to focus in particular on their character's perception of the excavation of the Foxes' den.

### LESSON 3

The major focus is once again on the main characters. What are they like? What qualities do they have? Provide time for the class to objectively evaluate each of them.

### Procedure

Read chapter 5 without comment. At the end of the chapter discuss the obsession of the farmers with Mr Fox's death. Why do they want to kill him so badly? Suggest to the students that they create a 'wanted' poster (see Johnson & Louis 1985) for Mr Fox. Show an example of a wanted poster and discuss its features. When the posters are completed allow students to share them before they are displayed on the wall.

Read chapters 6 and 7 and prepare character rating scales (see Johnson & Louis 1985) for Boggis, Bunce, Bean and Mr Fox. As a class complete one using the quality of intelligence.

### *Rating scale for 'Fantastic Mr Fox' — Intelligence*

Break the class into groups of two to three to complete other scales for the qualities of kindness and cunning. Allow the groups to come up with one or two qualities of their own.

When the groups have had sufficient time, ask them to share their responses, giving reasons for their ratings.

**Follow-up activities**

Allow time for students to complete their diary entries for the characters selected.

## LESSON 4

The primary focus of this lesson is to strengthen student engagement in the plot as the excitement grows within the story. They will be encouraged to predict what Mr Fox's plan will be, and to think about the likely success of his efforts, heightening involvement in the story.

**Procedure**

Read chapters 8 and 9.

Break the class into groups of three to five to discuss Mr Fox's plan. What will he do? What would you do in such a situation? Some children might want to use drawing or drama to show what they think will happen. If so, allow them to do so. Provide time for each group to share their thoughts, drawings and dramatic presentations.

**Follow-up activities**

Allow students to continue their diaries.

## LESSON 5

The major aim is to help students gain a greater understanding of the characters. More specifically, an attempt will be made to encourage the students to project themselves into the story, and the situation with which the Foxes are faced.

**Procedure**

Read chapters 10 and 11.

Ask students to comment on their predictions in the last lesson about Mr Fox's plan. How accurate were they? Will his plan be successful?

Break the class up into pairs and provide a copy of the dialogue between one of the children and Mrs Fox when Mr Fox returned with a chicken. Ask each pair to dramatise the scene of utter disbelief as Mrs Fox awakes to see food at last. Provide an opportunity for some of the pairs to present the dialogue in front of the class.

**Follow-up activities**

Allow students to continue their diaries. Because some of the students have characters who are not featured in these chapters provide them with the option of not adding an entry to their diaries. Alternatively, they might write an entry dealing with content not within the story. Stress to them that the entry should be consistent with the character and the plot. For example, Boggis, Bunce or Bean might write about the progress of the digging, and their feelings about the progress.

## LESSON 6

This lesson is primarily a time for reading. However, a discussion will be held concerning Bunce's storehouse to give students a greater appreciation of the events of these chapters.

**Procedure**

Read chapters 12 to 13.

After the reading provide time for the class to discuss the story. What do you think of Mr Fox's plan so far? Will it work? Could he be caught? How dangerous is the action he's taking?

Spend some time after this discussing Bunce's storehouse. Why did farmers have these storehouses? What were they like? What would they smell like? Encourage them to draw a picture of the storehouse. Share these in small groups of two to four students.

**Follow-up activities**

Allow your students to continue their diaries. Provide time for them in this lesson to share some of the entries they have been writing with other classmates.

## LESSON 7

Once again, this lesson is designed to heighten engagement in the story. Students will be encouraged to predict what will happen next to increase their involvement with the reading. As well, there will be an attempt to examine the character of Mrs Bean and consider Dahl's ability to create gross characters.

**Procedure**

a) Read chapters 14, 15 and part of 16. Stop at the point where Mrs Bean lifts a jar of cider right next to Mr Fox.

   Encourage the class to predict what will happen. Could this be the end for Mr Fox? Will his plan be uncovered and the food source cut off? Encourage them to use sketch to stretch to show what is going to happen.

   Allow time for students to share their ideas in groups of two to three, then read the rest of the chapter to see how accurate their predictions have been.

b) Read the section of Dahl's book *Boy* (1988) which describes Mrs Pratchett (pp.33-4). Ask them to see if they can identify any parallels between Mrs Pratchett and Mrs Bean. Allow time for the students to discuss each of these characters.

**Follow-up activities**

Encourage students to continue their diaries.

## LESSON 8

The major purpose is to complete the story and permit students to review the plot from the different characters' perspectives. How might each have viewed the events differently?

**Procedure**

Read chapters 17 and 18.

Allow time for the class to respond in general terms to the story. Were they pleased with the ending? Did they feel sorry for Boggis, Bunce and Bean? Would Mr Fox and his family be safe now?

Interview With Mr Fox

**Interviewer:** I'd like viewers to welcome Mr Fox to our studios this evening. Perhaps you could tell the viewers Mr Fox why you've been nicknamed 'Fantastic Mr Fox".

**Mr Fox:** Well it's a bit embarrassing really it was due to me outsmarting those disgusting farmers Boggis, Bunce and Bean.

**Interviewer:** How did this all happen?

**Mr Fox:** Well, for no apparent reason this charming trio decided to exterminate us. Just because we 'borrowed' the odd chicken, duck, goose or turkey.

**Interviewer:** What did they do?

**Mr Fox:** Well at first they tried to shoot me as my stumpy tail indicates. After that failed, they tried to dig us all out with bulldozers

**Interviewer:** So how did you outsmart them?

**Mr Fox:** Oh, it was easy really. After all, they aren't very bright. I simply tunneled down to their farms so we had a permanent food supply and the rest was up to them. They had no trouble making fools of themselves.

**Interviewer:** Well, that's quite a story Fantastic Mr Fox, thank you for sharing it with us.

**Mr Fox:** The pleasure was all mine, thank you

*A sample interview written in response to the book 'Fantastic Mr Fox'*

Once all students have been given an opportunity to respond, encourage them to draw the underground system of tunnels that the Foxes created. Ask your students to show how it is connected with the farms and to label all parts.

As a conclusion to the program invite your students to conduct an interview with either Boggis, Bunce, Bean or one of the Foxes. Break the class into pairs and ask one of the students to act as interviewer and one to act as the character. Encourage them to prepare a series of questions that will provide an insight into the character's perceptions of the events in the story.

## Follow-up activities

Ask all students to write a final entry in their diaries which shows how he/she feels about the ultimate outcome of the battle between the farmers and the Foxes. Provide time at the end of the lesson for students to share the diaries in pairs.

CHAPTER TWELVE

# Dear Mr Henshaw

**Literature:**   *Dear Mr Henshaw* (1983), Beverly Cleary
**Suggested Level:**   Grades three to five

## SYNOPSIS

This Newberry Medal winning book tells the story of a fourth grade boy's inner struggle to accept life without his father following his parents' separation. Through a series of letters and diary entries written by Leigh, both to himself and his favourite children's author (Mr Henshaw), we gain an insight into the boy's life.

## PROGRAM FOCUS

The major aims of this program are to:

a) Explore the way Leigh Botts learns to deal with the separation of his parents and his own emotions of anger, fear, isolation, loneliness and the need to be loved.

b) Encourage students to reflect upon Leigh's experiences and compare these with their own experiences.

c) Discuss the role writing plays in Leigh's emotional and personal growth.

d) Examine the way Cleary uses everyday incidents to amuse and engage us as readers.

## POSSIBLE LESSONS

### LESSON 1

The major purposes of this lesson are to engage the students in the story, discuss the central character (Leigh Botts) and encourage students to reflect upon their own reading experiences.

### Procedure

Begin reading the book stopping at the end of Leigh's letter of November 16th. Allow time for the students to offer their first reactions to this story. Do they like it? Does it remind them of other stories? Ask them to share any parts that they found amusing. Why? What is Leigh like? Is he like anyone they know?

Break the class into groups of four to six students and ask them to discuss the importance of *Ways to Amuse a Dog*. Why does it have so much significance for him? Encourage the groups to share the names of books that have been special for them and that they have read more than once. Ask them to think about the reasons their book was so special. Create a 'Great Books We Have Read...' chart to display in the classroom.

### Follow-up activities

Some students might like to look more closely at the letters that Leigh wrote. Get them to write down the way he signed each letter. Ask them to discuss the way the tone changed. Why might this have happened?

Other students might like to consider the questions Leigh asked of Boyd Henshaw. If they were writing to their favourite author what type of questions would they ask?

## LESSON 2

This lesson attempts to help students focus on the setting and begin to examine how Leigh's one sided relationship is developing with Mr Henshaw. As well, the students will be encouraged to predict Mr Henshaw's personality and character.

### Procedure

Continue reading the book without interruption, stopping as Leigh finishes answering his fifth question with the signature 'Pooped Writer'.

After the reading, allow time for the students to respond to the story in their own way. Move the focus of the discussion (if necessary) to Mr Henshaw. What type of person does he seem to be? Why did he ask Leigh so many questions? How would the students have answered each question? Perhaps re-read question 4 and invite the students to try and visualise Leigh's home and its setting. Allow time for them to draw the house and its surroundings.

## LESSON 3

The major purpose of this lesson is to probe more deeply into the character of Leigh Botts. The students will be encouraged to make speculations concerning his inner thoughts and feelings.

### Procedure

Begin this lesson by continuing the reading, stopping at the end of his letter of December 4th. Begin the discussion of this section of the story by asking the students to indicate how Mr Henshaw might feel about Leigh's letters to him.

Following this initial discussion break the class into groups of four to six students and ask them to discuss the ninth question that Leigh had to answer for Mr Henshaw – 'What bothers you?' Ask each group to consider what Mr Henshaw was getting at, then consider how they might answer the question. Have each group record these responses and share them with the whole class when the discussion has finished.

### One student's response to Mr Henshaw's question 'What bothers you?'

- Wars bother me
- Alsatian dogs bother me
- Homework bothers me
- Carol _____ bothers me
- Spiders bother me
- Angry teachers bother me
- Thinking about mom getting older bothers me
- Darkness bothers me
- Strong winds bother me

### Follow-up activities

As a follow-up to this lesson suggest to some students that they might like to think about Mr Henshaw's last question - 'What do you wish?' Encourage them to make a list of their ten major wishes.

### LESSON 4

The major purpose of this lesson is to encourage the class to think more deeply about the relationship Leigh has with his father and to examine the father's character.

### Procedure

Begin this lesson by reading to the end of Leigh's December 21st letter. At this point ask the class to suggest why Mr Henshaw has suggested Leigh keep a diary. Would it be a useful idea for Leigh? Why or why not?

Continue the reading of the book stopping at the end of his December 25th entry. Ask the class to discuss the significance of Leigh's reaction to his father's present, his relationship to him, and his father's character. Why was the gift so important to him? Suggest that the students think about the most special gift they ever received. Provide time for them to write about it. What was the gift? Who was it from? Why was it so special?

### Follow-up activities

As a follow-up to this lesson discuss with the class the role that diaries play. If the students do not already keep a diary encourage them to do so. Perhaps consider providing a lined book and a set period each day, to complete their diary entries.

## LESSON 5

This lesson aims to help students relate their own experiences to Leigh's, and empathise with the predicament he finds himself in as his lunch is continually stolen.

### Procedure

Continue reading the novel stopping at the end of the January 10th entry. Break the class into groups to discuss Leigh's problem of the disappearing lunches. Encourage the students to think about how they would feel if it happened to them and to share similar school experiences.

Encourage the groups to discuss Leigh's first solution to the problem and explore how they would have handled the problem.

## LESSON 6

This lesson will continue to examine the complex character of Leigh Botts and encourage students to uncover his basic needs for love and a sense of belonging. Doing this will also attempt to help students discuss Leigh's inner struggles to understand why his father has left home.

### Procedure

Continue reading the novel stopping at the end of the January 20th diary entry. Ask the class to think about Leigh's statement that Mr Fridley was 'so nice, sort of baggy and comfortable.' Would he have described his father as 'baggy and comfortable'? Why or why not? After the students have shared their interpretation of this statement encourage them to think about someone they know who is 'baggy and comfortable.' Have them share their reasons for selecting their person with the rest of the class.

Continue the reading until the end of the February 2nd diary entry. Break the class into groups of four to six students and ask them to discuss Leigh's mother's claim that his father was 'in love with his truck.' What did she mean? Ask the groups to record their responses and suggest other ways people can seemingly 'love' inanimate objects.

### Follow-up activities

Some students might like to write a letter from Leigh to his father challenging him to give up his truck and return home.

## LESSON 7

The major purpose of this lesson is to help students empathise with Leigh as he learns to accept his father as he is, and begins to realise his father's shortcomings.

### Procedure

Read Leigh's diary entry for February 4th without interruption. At the end of the reading break the class into groups of four to six and ask them to consider two things:

- How would Leigh have felt as he talked to his father?
- What would your reaction have been if you were Leigh and had discovered that Bandit had been lost?

After this discussion some students might practise and present a dramatic reading of the phone conversation between Leigh and his father. To do this it will be necessary to type and duplicate this section of the text, making sure each separate piece of dialogue, and each comment from the narrator is started on a new line.

### Follow-up activities

As a follow-up to this lesson invite students to prepare a poster to be placed in truck stops that would help to get Bandit back.

## LESSON 8

This lesson is primarily uninterrupted reading. As well, some limited time would be provided for discussion to allow students to continue to examine the problems Leigh's parents have experienced in their relationship.

### Procedure

Read the diary entry for February 5th without interruption.

Following the reading provide time for students to respond in general terms, then suggest that they discuss the problems Leigh's parents had experienced, as well as Leigh's growing awareness of, and acceptance of, their difficulties.

**Note** This would not be discussed with younger students.

## LESSON 9

As well as continuing the reading of the novel, this lesson aims to heighten engagement with the plot (using discussion and drawing), and encourage students to reflect upon the writing difficulties of Leigh and Mr Henshaw. Students would be encouraged to consider the latter in the light of their own experiences as writers.

### Procedure

Read Leigh's diary entry for February 7th. Following the reading break the class into pairs to discuss Leigh's problem with his disappearing lunches. Have all students discuss how he might design an alarm system. Encourage everyone to draw a picture of the alarm that he might make.

After the students have shared the designs for Leigh's alarm continue the reading of the novel to the end of Leigh's February 28th diary entry. Break the class into groups of three to four students and encourage them to discuss the troubles Leigh and Mr Henshaw experience with writing. Ask each student to share his/her struggles, listing each for later sharing with the complete class.

## LESSON 10

The primary purpose of this lesson is to provide an opportunity for students to discover how Leigh solves the problem of the lunch thief, and to consider other solutions to his problem.

## LOST

### Black dog

← bandanna

Where: On Highway 80 near a Truck Stop in Colorado

Description: Black, friendly answers to name Bandit. Wearing a red bandanna instead of a collar.

Special features: Howls when music is played. Loves trucks.

Contact: Leigh Botts,
Ocean Rd,
Pacific Grove, California.
Phone 929 6124.

## REWARD!

*A lost and found poster that Leigh might place in truck stops to try and find Bandit*

Bell

Wire joined to lid. When lifted pulls loop of wire up to touch nail

Lunch box
alarm

One student's dra-
wing of what Leigh's
lunch alarm might
look like

## Procedure

Continue the reading stopping at the end of the March 15th diary entry. Provide time for the class to discuss Leigh's efforts to stop the lunch thief. Would they have done it the same way? What other solutions were possible? Why was Leigh pleased he never found out who the thief was?

## Follow-up activities

Some students might like to explore the other solutions that Leigh could have used to stop the lunch thief. Encourage the students to describe their techniques in report form, or simply draw design plans for each idea.

It might also be possible to provide time for students to share experiences they had at school, that at the time, seemed just as serious as Leigh's problem.

## LESSON 11

The major purpose of the discussion in this lesson will be to focus on the relationship between Leigh and his father. In particular, students will be encouraged to consider Leigh's growing insecurity as he realises his father has another life, and another family.

> Monday, March 26
>
> I can't stop thinking about my mum and dad. Why can't they get on like lots of other parents?! It's a bit rough when your dad loves his truck better than you. I wish my dad was a plumber you can't love a bunch of pipes.
> I just wish we could all be together again — me, dad, mum and bandit. Sometimes I think I hate him.

*A sample diary entry for Leigh in which he reflects upon his deteriorating relationship with his father*

### Procedure

Continue reading the novel to the end of the diary entry for March 25th. As a class discuss Leigh's growing insecurity. Why is he feeling insecure? Are his fears justified? Ask the students to consider how they would react. Finally, suggest that they write an additional diary entry for Leigh in which he bares more of his inner turmoil about his deteriorating relationship with his father.

### LESSON 12

Within the reading for this lesson Leigh learns a number of lessons concerning himself as a writer. The major focus within the discussion that follows will be upon the insights that are gained about writing.

### Procedure

Continue the reading of the novel to the end of the diary entry of March 30th. Provide time for the class to discuss the things Leigh learns about himself as a writer. Ask the students to write down what they consider the most important lesson that Leigh learned. How did the author (Mrs Badger) help him?

As a class select several favourite authors and write to them asking a number of basic questions:

- What is your single most important reason for writing?
- What do you find hardest about writing?
- What do you find easiest?
- Do you remember anyone or anything that particularly helped you to improve as a writer?
- What is the most important piece of advice that you could give to young writers?

## Follow-up activities

As a follow-up to this lesson you might consider organising a writing competition for the class or school. You might create specific categories for the competition (e.g. poetry, prose, factual, autobiographical etc) and select a well known writing identity to act as the judge.

## LESSON 13

This is the last lesson in the program so it will provide an opportunity for students to respond to the novel in a variety of ways. A major focus in the discussion that follows the reading will be the nature of Leigh's relationship with his parents, and the lessons he has learned about both.

### Procedure

Complete the reading of the novel. After the reading break the class into groups of four to six students. Provide the groups with a number of questions designed to help them reflect upon the things Leigh has learned about himself and his relationship with his mother and father. For example: How does Leigh now feel about his father? Has his attitude towards him changed? Why or why not? How does Leigh's mother feel about her husband? What is the significance of Leigh letting his father keep Bandit? What did Leigh mean in the final lines of the book '...I felt sad and a whole lot better at the same time?'

Following this discussion ask the students to write in their own words how they might feel if they were Leigh Botts. This could take a variety of forms, e.g. a letter to the father, a diary entry, or simply a list.

### Follow-up activities

Some (older) students might like to write a poem expressing something of Leigh's loneliness and sadness as he struggles with life without his father. This might be in a modified cinquain form such as the following:

        _____All alone,

        _____2 words expressing how he feels,

        _____3 words indicating his hopes,

        _____2 words expressing his fears,

        _____A synonym for 'all alone'.

CHAPTER THIRTEEN

# The Pinballs

**Literature:** *The Pinballs*, Betsy Byars
**Suggested Level:** Grades three to five

## SYNOPSIS

*The Pinballs* (1977) is the story of three abused and neglected children who find themselves thrown together with a loving 'childless' couple, who have devoted themselves to a total of seventeen foster children over the years. Byars tells of the slow bonding process of timid Thomas J., an immobile and despondent Harvey, and the cynical and sarcastic Carlie. After an initial period of rebellion and indifference, Carlie's 'rat cunning', resilience and love leave their mark on all members of the Mason household.

## PROGRAM FOCUS

The major purposes in treating this novel are to:
a) Concentrate on some of the themes that Byars has developed. For example, the basic human need for security, love and a sense of belonging, dealing with disappointments in life, the human desire for hope and trust.
b) Examine the way Byars uses language to create strong images.
c) Encourage students to empathise with the major characters.

## POSSIBLE LESSONS

### LESSON 1

This lesson aims primarily to engage the students in the story. As well, discussions will centre on the personalities of the major characters introduced.

**Procedure**

Commence the program with the reading of chapters 1 and 2.

After the reading break the class into groups of two to four to discuss the three main characters. The groups might discuss the lives the three characters have had — who has had the toughest childhood? Why? As well, encourage your students to consider how the children might get on. Why might Harvey have lied to Carlie about the cause of his broken legs?

**Follow-up activities**

As a follow-up to the above discussion you might ask your students to write a literary journal entry (see Johnson & Louis 1985) for Carlie or Harvey, describing their first day in the Mason house. Stress to your students that it is important to write it as if they are the character, and to think about the type of things the character would say.

*Sample journal entry*

Dear Journal,

After one day in this dump I'm ready to get out. The wrinklies who've taken me in are right out of the ark. What's more I'm locked up here with a cripple and a wimp who won't say boo. Mrs Mason seems to smile about everything, but I'll soon put a stop to that when I get into my stride. Give me a week and they'll be begging the authorities to take me back.

Carlie

**LESSON 2**

The main focus is on the four major characters — Thomas J., Harvey, Carlie and Mrs Mason. The use of character rating scales provides a valuable vehicle to discuss the qualities of each of these key figures in the novel.

## Procedure

Start by reading chapters 3 to 5 without comment.

After chapter 5 ask the students to list the main characters introduced so far. What do you think of them? Do they remind you of people you know? Brainstorm some of their qualities.

Introduce the use of character rating scales. Explain that they are a means to discuss the qualities of characters in relation to specific personality traits. Choose a characteristic (e.g. honesty versus dishonesty) and demonstrate how it is possible to rate characters on this quality.

Ask students to complete rating scales for the following characteristics: confident — timid, kind — unkind, intelligent — unintelligent.

When groups have finished rating the characters, ask them to share the responses and attempt to record consensus of opinion on the overhead or board.

### *Consensus of Ratings for a Group of Grade 3–5 Students*

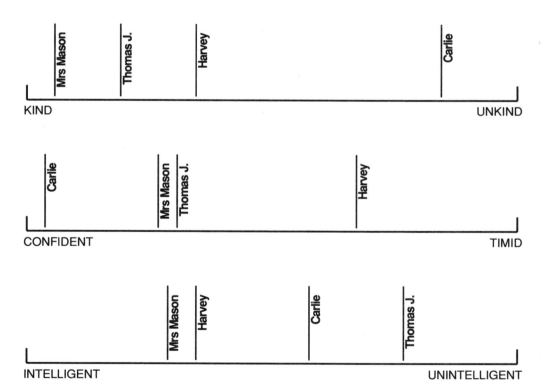

## Follow-up activities

As an extension to the previous character rating lesson ask your students to choose several qualities of their own and apply them to all characters. At the conclusion of the lesson ask them to share with the class the qualities they have chosen and the ratings they have given for each character.

## LESSON 3

This lesson is concerned mainly with a discussion of Carlie's claim that as foster children they are just like pinballs. This is not only a pointer to the title of the book, it is a clue to an important theme that dominates the book — all people need to be loved and feel secure, we all need to 'belong'.

### Procedure

Start by reading chapter 6.

At the end of the chapter break the class into groups of two to four to consider Carlie's description of them as 'pinballs'.

> Harvey and me and Thomas J. are just like pinballs. Somebody put in a dime and punched a button and out we came, ready or not, and settled in the same groove. That's all.

What does she mean?

Bring the groups back together for a sharing time as a class.

## LESSON 4

The major purpose is to encourage students to focus on the lack of security and love the central characters have experienced. As well, an attempt will be made to examine the role that writing plays in maintaining relationships, and to relate this back to the desire of Carlie, Thomas J. and Harvey to feel 'they belong' to someone.

### Procedure

Read chapters 7 and 8 without comment.

After the reading provide an opportunity for your students to respond in general terms to the text. After this encourage them to discuss the importance that letters can play in the maintenance of relationships. How important are personal letters to them? Can they recall receiving any special letters? How important were letters to Harvey, Thomas J. and Carlie? Why?

Offer the class one of three invitations to use writing to respond to the chapter:

a) Write a letter from Carlie to her mother pleading to be taken home (perhaps re-read the relevant part of the story.

b) Write a letter as one of the three main characters describing the home. Harvey and Carlie might write to their mothers, while Thomas J. could write to the Benson Twins. Before starting the writing discuss how the letters might be different.

c) Motivated by Harvey's 'list writing' ask the students to write a list about themselves. For example, 'Bad Things that Have Happened to Me', 'Good Things that Have Happened to Me', 'People I'm Most Afraid Of', 'Books I Have Enjoyed', 'Promises My Mother Broke'. Some might prefer to make up their own list rather than following Harvey's lead.

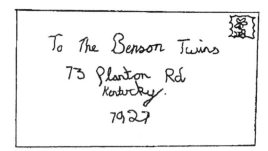

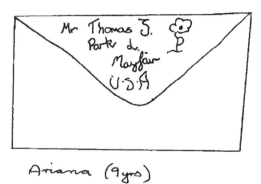

Dear ♦ Aunty's Benson X
How are your hips. ⚘
I miss you. When you
get better please come and
pick me up. I am with Mrs
Mason and 2 other Kids
Carlie the oldest is bossy
and Harvey has 2
broken legs. I wish
to come ___ and see
the house again
get well ♡ love
your little boy
~~Benson~~
Thomas J.

RJ I love you,
the cooking great, and
Mrs Mason has brought
17 kids ⚘ wow

To The Benson Twins
73 Planton Rd
Kentucky.
7927

Mr Thomas J.
Parke d.
Mayfair
U·S·A

Ariana (9yrs)

*A letter written by Ariana (aged 9 yrs) to the Benson Twins*

## LESSON 5

The purpose is to encourage students to identify the inner problems of Harvey, Thomas J. and Carlie. In particular, the discussion of the chapters will give an insight into the basic human need to 'belong' which we see so clearly demonstrated through Harvey.

### Procedure

Read chapters 9 to 11 without comment.

At the end of the reading break the class into groups of four to six to discuss Thomas J.'s feelings as he watches the Benson twins 'dying'. How must he have felt? Why? Why did Thomas J. suddenly want to know about the day the twins first found him?

Bring the class back together to share their thoughts, then discuss with the class group the disappointment that Harvey felt when they arrived back without the chicken. Why was he so disappointed? Why would the memory of eating chicken alone in a home where he was mistreated by a drunken father have positive associations for Harvey? Try to get the students to discuss the importance that a sense of 'belonging' has for people.

## LESSON 6

The purpose is to probe more deeply into the character of Harvey. Specifically, the discussions will look at the disappointments he has experienced and the effect they have had upon him.

### Procedure

Read chapter 12 without comment.

Ask the students to break into groups of two to three to discuss the chapter. What are some of the disappointments that Harvey has had? What is the common thread in all these disappointments?

After the chapter has been discussed encourage students to recall and discuss any big disappointments in their lives. What were they? Have the groups share some of these memories. Attempt to get the groups to examine the consequences of disappointments, that is, answer the question — What happens when we are constantly disappointed? Attempt to get the groups to look at the effect on the individual, as well as relationships with those who disappoint you.

## LESSON 7

The aim is to examine the bond that is starting to develop between Carlie, Harvey and Thomas J. Why is it developing? What are the characters beginning to recognise in each other?

### Procedure

Read chapters 13 and 14.

Following the reading ask for general responses to the chapters. How do you feel about Carlie at this point in the story compared with the early parts of the story? Do you still see Carlie in the same way, or can you see that she has changed? If the group agrees there has been change, ask them to discuss the nature of the changes they have identified.

Break the class into groups of four to six to consider why Harvey has suddenly decided to tell Carlie the real story about his broken legs. What does this indicate about their relationship?

Re-read the section of chapter 13 where Harvey tells Carlie the truth. To do this you will need to have this section of text typed, separating each line of dialogue for the specific characters and placing all comments by the narrator in brackets. Ask students in pairs to dramatise this scene using only the dialogue from the two characters.

### Follow-up activities

As a follow-up, ask students to predict the type of father Harvey would have wanted. Re-read the last five to six paragraphs of chapter 13 where Carlie contemplates what it would be like to be able to decide as a baby, 'What I want in a father'.

## LESSON 8

The aim is to encourage students to look more closely at the complex character of Harvey. What are his inner hopes and aspirations?

### Procedure

Read chapter 15.

After the reading ask students to discuss Harvey's idea that everyone in life will be famous for fifteen minutes. What is the significance of this comment? Why might it be an encouragement to Harvey?

FAMOUS for 15 minutes

POP STAR    FAMOUS BASE BALL Player & Basket ball player cricketer Tennis player    movie star    inventer Artist    poetest    desiner    Stock bracker inventing a car as fast as Lightning Swimmer    Loyar    Book writer

Darren (9yrs)

*Darren's response to an invitation to write how he would like to be famous for fifteen minutes*

### Follow-up activities

As a follow-up, ask your students to form pairs and brainstorm the ways in which they might become famous for fifteen minutes. Bring the class back together and ask individual students to share responses.

### LESSON 9

The focus within this lesson is on the language that Byars uses. In particular, students would be encouraged to examine Byars' use of simile. What is a simile, and how does the author use them?

### Procedure

Start by indicating to the class that you intend examining the language Byars uses in her novel. Remind them of the discussion in a previous lesson of Carlie's statement that the children were just like 'pinballs'. Ask them once more to recall what she meant by this statement and point out that this use of language is in fact a simile.

Highlight other examples of Byars' use of simile in the chapters read so far. For example, 'He felt as flat as an old tyre. He could hardly wheel himself into his room'. How did Harvey feel? Why? Why does Byars say it this way? Introduce the class to a number of half-written similes and have them complete them in pairs. At the completion of this activity have specific students share the similes they have written.

### Sample similes for group work

Complete the following similes:

I felt as cold as . . . . . . . . . . . . . . . . . . . . . . . . . . . . . . . . . . . . . . . .

She was as thin as . . . . . . . . . . . . . . . . . . . . . . . . . . . . . . . . . . . . . .

His hands were as rough as . . . . . . . . . . . . . . . . . . . . . . . . . . . . . . .

Carol finished the race breathing like . . . . . . . . . . . . . . . . . . . . . . . .

## LESSON 10

This lesson aims primarily to encourage students to discuss the growing bond between the Masons (in this case Mr Mason) and the children (in this case Thomas J.). What are the Masons offering the children that they have never had before?

### Procedure

Read chapters 17 and 18 up to the point where it says Thomas J. '...felt like somebody out of a book, a fairy tale, who had just stepped into real life and needed to know about it. He said to Mr Mason, "Tell me some more about the things that happened to you when you were little"'.

Break the class into groups of four to six students and ask them to discuss how Thomas J. must have felt. What did he mean? What did he need to know?

Finish reading chapter 18 and all of chapter 19.

### Follow-up activities

As an extension to the above you might consider stopping the reading of chapter 19 to use sketch to stretch at the point just before Carlie reveals what Harvey is going to get for his birthday. Ask your students to predict what the present might be and to quickly sketch it. When using this strategy always stress that the quality of the sketch is unimportant. Once the sketches are complete ask specific students to share the predictions.

## LESSON 11

The aim is primarily to continue the reading of the book, encouraging engagement with the plot. As well, there will be discussion of Carlie and Thomas J.'s gift to Harvey. This is designed to promote links with previous chapters. In particular, it is hoped that all students can relate the birthday gift to previous disappointments that Harvey has had in life (e.g. his guinea pig, Snowball).

### Procedure

Read chapters 20 and 21.

At the end of chapter 21 indicate that Carlie has plans to do more than simply make a cake for Harvey. Ask the students to predict how Carlie might do this. What other special gift might she give him? Get them to either brainstorm a list of possibilities or simply draw what Carlie might choose for him.

**Possible Gifts that Carlie might give to Harvey**

A white Guinea Pig

Louise (9 yrs)

Before in the story Harvey went out and bought a guinea Pig for his birthday present and his father threw it out.

Kylie (10 yrs)

I think a dog is an ideal gift for Harvey. A loving playful puppy would be wonderful company

*Sample sketches of gifts that Harvey might have enjoyed receiving*

## LESSON 12

The aim will be to encourage the students to discuss the full significance of the gift of the puppy. Why was it so special? What were they able to achieve by giving this special gift?

## Procedure

Read chapters 22 and 23.

At the end of the reading break the class into groups of four to six to discuss the following questions:

- How do these chapters make you feel? Why?
- Why did the nurse ignore the dog? What did she realise?
- What do you think Mrs Mason will say about the gift?
- What had Carlie and Thomas J. really given Harvey? Was it just another pet present? Why might this present have been so special?
- Can you recall a time when you received a gift that had a similar impact on you, that was more than 'just a present'?

## Follow-up activities

As a follow-up some students might like to write about their special present.

## LESSON 13

The major purpose is to complete the novel, allowing time for reflection. It is hoped that students will also be able to project their own emotions into the story and to evaluate it as a work of literature.

## Procedure

Read chapters 24 to 26.

At the conclusion of the book allow time for the group to respond to it in their own way. Some might like to share their feelings about the story, the characters, the ending. Others might like to compare it with other books they have read.

Once general responses have been exhausted ask the class to discuss in groups of two to four what for them is the significance of the last line: 'Let's go home'.

## Follow-up activities

a) As an alternative to the previous lesson format stop the reading soon after starting chapter 26, at the point where Carlie says:

"You know, Thomas J.," she said, "wouldn't it be nice if we could get to our brains with an eraser?"
"What?" He looked at her, puzzled. "Did you say eraser?"
"Yeah. I just mean that there are things I don't like to remember — oh, like times people snubbed me at school — times people made me feel bad — and if I could just erase those things, Thomas J., I'd be a lot happier."

Break the class into groups of two to four and ask them to consider what Thomas J., Carlie and Harvey might 'rub out'. As well, they might share memories they have that they would gladly 'rub out'.

b) You might suggest to your students that they consider reading *The Great Gilly Hopkins* (Paterson 1987) because of the similarity of the major characters (Carlie and Gilly) and storyline. Alternatively suggest other Betsy Byars books, which they might read e.g. *The Eighteenth Emergency* (1973).

CHAPTER FOURTEEN                                          # Boy

**Literature:**   *Boy*, Roald Dahl
**Suggested Level:**   Grades five to seven

## SYNOPSIS

*Boy* (1988) is a true story of Dahl's childhood. It is a collection of stories arranged in chronological sequence. Many are funny, some are sad, and others slightly grotesque, but always they force the reader to reflect upon the agonies of being a child. It is a patchwork of experiences painted against a kaleidoscope of people and places compelling the reader to relive his/her own childhood as Dahl's is explored.

## PROGRAM FOCUS

The major reasons for studying *Boy* are to help students:
a) More fully appreciate the way Dahl creates colourful characters and believable relationships.
b) Reflect upon their childhood experiences projecting them into the story, as well as contrasting them with Dahl's.
c) Gain a greater insight into a childhood world between the two 'great wars'.
d) Reflect upon the language Dahl uses to amuse, shock and entertain; see the text as a springboard for experimentation with a variety of written genres.
e) Compare their own and their parents' childhoods with Dahl's.
f) Learn the distinctive features of autobiographical writing.

## POSSIBLE LESSONS

### LESSON 1
The purpose of this lesson is to introduce the novel and the genre of autobiography.

**Procedure**

Before reading *Boy* briefly discuss with the class books they have already read that were written by Dahl. Did they like or dislike them, why, or why not? Explain that *Boy* is a collection of true stories from Dahl's childhood before reading Dahl's introduction that outlines his claim that *Boy* is not an autobiography.

Next, briefly discuss their understanding of the term autobiography, and discuss how this book is different. End the lesson with the reading of the first chapter.

**Follow-up activities**

As a follow-up you might arrange a display of autobiographical material, perhaps reading segments from each.

## LESSON 2

This lesson aims to establish greater knowledge of the period in which Dahl's memories are set, and to encourage students to relate their experiences to those shared by Dahl.

**Procedure**

Start by reading chapters 2 and 3.

At the end of chapter 3, suggest to the class that they ask their parents about the lollies Dahl describes. Encourage them to talk to their parents (or grandparents) that evening to see if they can remember what sherbert suckers, acid drops, all day suckers and liquorice bootlaces were like.

As well, ask your students to record anything interesting their parents recall, and bring these points along to share the next day.

**Follow-up activities**

As a follow-up you might encourage your pupils to conduct their own survey of tastes in sweets. What are the most popular sweets today? Are there any of Dahl's favourites still available? If so, are they the same? How do prices, packaging etc. vary for sweets today?

### *Our Favourite Sweets* (In order)

1. Mars Bars.

2. Crunchies.

3. Popcorn.

## LESSON 3

The major focus is Dahl's ability to 'paint' wonderful pictures of his characters. Special attention will be given to the way Dahl describes these characters, and communicates details of personality as well as physical appearance.

## Procedure

Begin by reading chapter 4. The chapter tells the story of how Dahl and four of his friends plant a dead mouse in a sweet jar belonging to the dreaded Mrs Pratchett.

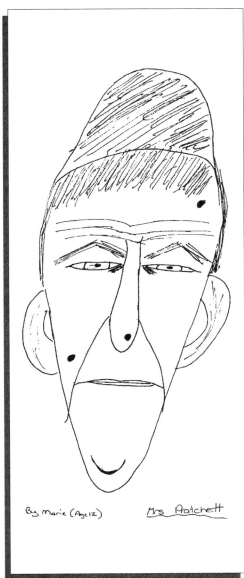

By Marie (Age 12)    Mrs Pratchett

*A sketch of Mrs Pratchett based on the book 'Boy'*

At the conclusion of this chapter discuss the events that occur and the characters introduced — What do you think of the 'great mouse plot'? Should they have done it? Will Mrs Pratchett find out who did it? I would encourage them to use sketch to stretch to explore what might occur next in the story, suggesting they try to visualise the scene, the consequences of the discovery, and the interaction of characters.

Share the sketches, asking students to explain what they have drawn and the details of their predictions. This is best done in small groups, but can be done as a class if desired.

### Follow-up activities

As a follow-up you might encourage some students to think about other 'plots' that could have been used to get back at Mrs Pratchett.

### LESSON 4

The major focus would again be on Dahl's great mastery of character portrayal. Why is he so effective? What devices does he use? Why are the characters so real?

### Procedure

Commence with the reading of chapters 5 and 6.

After chapter 6 is finished, break the class up into small groups of three to five and ask them to discuss Mrs Pratchett. What do they think of her? Was her moment of revenge justified? Did they have their own 'Mrs Pratchetts'? Encourage them to discuss these people. Why did they find them difficult to like?

Perhaps ask them to describe an incident involving their 'Mrs Pratchett'. What happened? How did they react? Read Dahl's descrip-

Lisa W (9 yrs)

Name: Mrs Pracheet
Alias: Prachie
Age: 107
Address: The Sweet stop
Description: fat small body (thin in manners)

Special Features: None

Major Goals in Life: To cheat little kids and be surfing with a boy who is 20
Unusual or Interesting Habits. Grimy hands and foul apron.

*A character mugsheet for Mrs Pratchett from the book 'Boy'*

description of her once more, and suggest that some people might want to write a short descriptive piece describing their own 'Mrs Pratchett'.

Once these descriptions have been shared in small groups, ask group members to select one for sharing with the whole class.

**Follow-up activities**

Perhaps finish the lesson by suggesting that some students might like to create a character mugsheet for their Mrs Pratchett.

## LESSON 5

The major focus is on the way in which Dahl describes the setting for chapters 7 and 8. How does he achieve this? To what extent does his description of setting go beyond the physical setting? How do people contribute to the sense of place?

**Procedure**

Read chapters 7 and 8 concerning Dahl's trips to Norway.

Following the reading, ask the class why Norway appeared to be such a special place to Dahl. Was it simply the place, or did it have even more to do with the people and the events of the holiday? After discussing this as a class invite them to explore one of the following options:

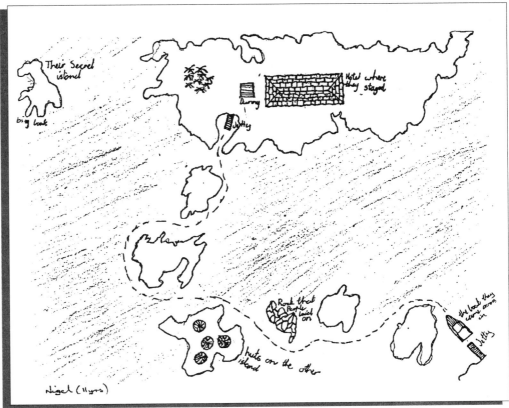

*Nigel's map of the Norwegian islands visited in the book 'Boy'*

a) Draw a map (see Johnson & Louis 1985; Cairney 1986) of the magic island. What might it have been like? What would the chain of islands have been like?

b) Recall the best holiday you can ever remember. Why was it so enjoyable? Write a brief description of an incident, person or place.

c) Imagine the perfect holiday. What would the place be like? How would you get there? Who would you go with? Where would you stay?

## LESSON 6

A major aim is to encourage students to learn more about living standards during the time period about which Dahl writes. In particular, they would be encouraged to compare the standard of health care offered then compared with the 1980s.

### Procedure

Start by reading chapter 9.

After the reading discuss the methods that were once used for operations, the lack of hospital facilities, the high mortality rate etc. Ask the students to try to imagine a time when there was no penicillin, and when measles, appendicitis and the common cold often killed.

Encourage them to talk to their grandparents about doctors and hospitals in their younger days, asking them to try to recall some of their most vivid memories. Ask them to record these memories either in note form or with a tape recorder. Bring them along the next day for sharing.

### Follow-up activities

Another option would be to dramatise the operation in the doctor's surgery as it was described by Dahl. Ask the students to pay special attention to the characters, and remind them that Dahl didn't know what to expect, but that his mother and the doctor did. Encourage the group to consider how this would affect their actions in the 'operating room'.

## LESSON 7

The major focus is the genre of personal letter writing. What are its special features? What functions do personal letters perform? How important are letters to them?

### Procedure

Begin by reading chapters 10 to 13.

Following the reading ask the students if they have ever written to their parents when away from home. What did they write about? How did they feel? Were they homesick? Encourage them to write a letter to someone they rarely see. What form should the letter take? What should be included in the letter? Make sure that all letters written are posted.

Dec 7th

Dear Mother,

This place is the bottoms. It's dark and cold and inhabited by the most horrible and fierce matron. Please come and rescue me. I don't think I can survive a day longer. She patrols the corridors waiting for us to do something wrong. We are vervim in her eyes waiting to be stomped by her giant feet. Mother, please, please save me !!!

Love,
Your dearly devoted son.

*Sample letter to Dahl's mother*

**Follow-up activities**

An alternative to this lesson would be to initiate a penfriend program with another class (preferably at a distance). Such a program is usually organised with the teacher of a compatible class who then passes on the names of students to whom your class can write. I usually have my students write their letters in school time. I collect them on a specific day each week, then post them off to the other teacher together in one large envelope. While this is slightly less personal, it is a much more reliable method. It is nevertheless a good idea to encourage your students to seal their letters in a small envelope that can be slipped inside a larger one.

## LESSON 8

The major focus is on the amusing way in which Dahl writes about something that could have been quite serious. Focus on the clever literary devices he uses.

### Procedure

Read chapter 14.

After a general discussion in which students are asked to respond to the content of the chapter spend extra time re-reading Dahl's description of the car accident.

After students have been given an opportunity to respond in general terms to the chapter, comment on Dahl's description of the event, and ask them to discuss the reaction of all the characters involved. How did each seem to feel and react? Ask the class to try to remember a time when they were hurt, encouraging them to think of the reaction of other people to their accident. Invite students to write about their incident if they wish.

## LESSON 9

Once again the focus is on characterisation. Dahl's description of Captain Hardcastle provides an excellent opportunity to examine the use of sarcasm as a form of humour. How effectively does Dahl use this device?

### Procedure

After reading chapter 15, discuss the central character, seeking general reactions. What did Dahl think of him? What makes you say this? Why might he have felt this way?

How does Dahl use sarcasm? What did he mean by '...even small insects like us knew that 'Captain' was not a very exalted rank and only a man with little else to boast about would hang on to it in civilian life. It was bad enough to keep calling yourself 'Major' after it was all over, but 'Captain' was the bottoms'. What other examples of this type of humour can be found?

### Follow-up activities

As a follow-up re-read the dialogue between Captain Hardcastle and the students asking to be excused from Prep. Suggest that your students might like to create similar dialogues (using the examples as models), writing them down and acting them out for the whole class.

**LESSON 10**

This lesson builds on the previous one, looking closely at Dahl's humour. What literary devices does he use to amuse the reader?

**Procedure**

Read chapters 16 and 17.

Talk briefly about the first chapter then discuss Dahl's practical joke with the goat's 'tobacco' at length. What would goat's tobacco taste like?

Discuss the names Dahl gives to the characters (i.e. 'the manly lover' and the 'ancient half-sister'). What do his names suggest about his feelings towards them? After this ask the class to think of people in their lives who have been unbearable. Some students could be encouraged to produce a character sketch for this person. What 'pet' names might Dahl have invented for them?

### Our Favourite 'Pet' Names

Speedy Gonzales
Grime grip
The shower slug
Acid tongue
Super snoop
Daddy's precious prune

**LESSONS 11 PLUS**

The major purpose of this and remaining lessons is to complete the reading of the book and permit the class to reflect on the complete work.

**Procedure**

Over perhaps four lessons read the remaining eight chapters without inviting the class to be involved in any activities. When the book has been completed hold a group sharing and brainstorming session in which the students are asked to form small groups and discuss the whole story.

Ask each group to list the things they liked and disliked about this book, things that reminded them of their own life, and things which surprised or puzzled them. Later come together as a class and share the ideas in each category. Finally, the class should be encouraged to respond to each other's ideas.

**Follow-up activities**

Many activities could arise from the final eight chapters but it would not be desirable to continue stretching out the treatment of the book. Nevertheless, several possible follow-up activities are worthy of mention:

a) Share the poem 'Hard Cheese' (*Junior Voices*, Summerfield 1970, Book 4, pp. 68-70), and draw parallels between its major theme and *Boy*. Invite general reactions from the class, before asking students to suggest what the poem might tell us: about parents, ourselves (children), about the 'games' we play at the expense of our parents (trying to fool, mislead). Conduct this as a brainstorming session either as a class or in small groups.

b) Suggest that the class interview their parents about their experiences at school. Ask them to share the things they remember most. Encourage them to tape the interviews, take notes and collect memorabilia. They should also ask their parents for any photographs they have for the period they are recalling, e.g. school photographs. Each child would prepare a presentation of one incident from their parents' lives. Over a period of perhaps a week the class would share these stories.

c) Finally, you could finish the work on *Boy* by talking about other biographies, autobiographies, or real stories of childhood e.g. *Helen Keller's Teacher* (Davidson 1972), *The Story of Louis Braille* (Davidson 1971), *Little House on the Prairie* (Wilder 1975). Read sections from each and encourage students to read one independently.

CHAPTER FIFTEEN
# The Machine-Gunners

**Literature:**  *The Machine-Gunners* (1975), Robert Westall
**Suggested Level:**  Grades six to eight

## SYNOPSIS

This story deals with the impact of World War II on a group of children living in the north of England. It tells of the daily lives of these young rogues who extend their war souvenir collection by adding a machine-gun taken secretly from a crashed German plane. The children set up a gun emplacement with the sole purpose of shooting down an enemy plane. The events that follow provide an enthralling adventure story. This book was winner of the Carnegie Medal in 1975.

## PROGRAM FOCUS

There is much that can be examined in this novel but within this program the major emphases will be:
a) An examination of the characters that Westall creates for us. What are their inner struggles and needs?
b) How does the novel provide an insight into the impact of war on children?
c) How are the problems these children face relevant to our lives?
d) How does Westall create such quality characters? What makes them so special?
e) What was life like during World War II? What were the secret fears, the burdens, the special outcomes of the conflict?

## POSSIBLE LESSONS

### LESSON 1

The aim is to engage the class in the story, and encourage students to link the experiences of Chas and the other principal characters with their lives.

**Procedure**

Before starting the story explain to the class that this story is set in the north of England in 1940-1 at a stage of the war when Germany was bombing English targets daily.

Read chapters 1 and 2.

Allow time for general responses to the story. What do you think of Chas, Boddser Brown, Cem and Audrey? Do they remind you of children you know? How might you have coped with life in the war? Do you like the story so far?

After initial responses of a general nature ask the class for their opinion of war souvenirs. Extend the discussion to their own collections — what do they collect? (See the list that one group compiled). How did they start collecting? Is there rivalry between collectors? What is their most prized item?

### Things We Collect

- Shells
- Badges
- Dolls
- Money
- Stamps
- Erasers
- Stickers
- Swap cards
- Comics
- Posters

**Follow-up activities**

As a follow-up you might ask your students to bring their collections to school to show other students. Perhaps the class could conduct a display of collections for the rest of the school.

## LESSON 2

The major focus is on the setting in which the story takes place. The story has a strong sense of place which is important to the events that are to take place in following chapters.

**Procedure**

Read chapters 3 to 5.

After providing time for responses of a general nature to the story ask students to draw a map of the area in which the story is set. Remind the class to include as many of the physical locations mentioned in the story as possible. For example, the plane in the woods, the children's houses, the hiding place for the machine gun, Bogie Lane, Willington Quay, the school.

Provide time for students to share the maps in small groups explaining why they have represented the area in this way.

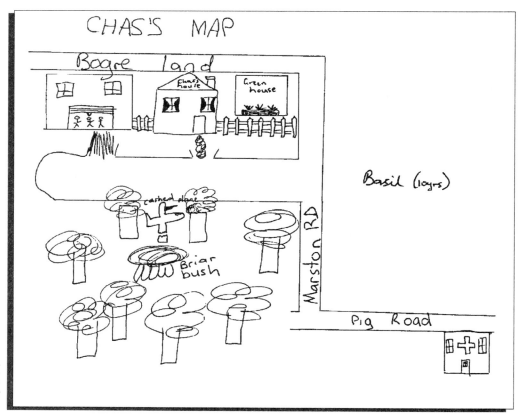

*A map of the character Chas' neighbourhood in 'The Machine-Gunners'*

### Follow-up activities

a) As an extension, some students might want to prepare a large wall frieze of the region in which the story is set.

b) Ask your students to consider whether it was morally right for Chas to take the machine-gun. Break the class into groups of four to six to brainstorm arguments for and against Chas taking the gun. You might even structure a formal debate between two sides, one for and one against the removal of the gun.

### LESSON 3

The focus is on the scene that accompanies daily air raids for Chas and his family. In particular, an attempt will be made to examine the almost unrealistic nature of the war experience for the people involved. While death was all around, people found it hard to see themselves as being personally affected.

### Procedure

Read the first five pages of chapter 6 stopping at the point where Chas describes the counting in which they engage as bombs fall, as a '...silly pointless game, with no real magic in it, but it stopped you wanting to scream...'

AIR RADES    By Basil (10 yrs)

crackling          graqdes blowing up
screaming          bang bang banging
exploding          people dying
chugging           Germans killing
scurrying          parachutes droping
crashing           plates breaking
banging            pets runing
runing             black outs
collapsing         petrified
shooting           cars exploding
crying             doors slamming
damaging           reol alert
dark
bombers bombing
windows shattering
houses collapsing
planes zooming through the sky

*One student's list of images written in response to 'The Machine-Gunners'*

There is an hilarious description of the family clambering to the air raid shelter, culminating with Mrs Spalding 'falling' through the door of the shelter with her 'knickers round her ankles'.

Discuss the incident, focusing on the frenzy of activity as everyone tries to get to the shelter and the seemingly irrational behaviour of Chas' mother. How could she be concerned about closing the door and getting the insurance policies at a time when they are faced with possible death? What does the behaviour of the characters show about their experience of the war?

Following this discussion ask students to close their eyes and imagine the sights, smells, sounds and things they might feel if they were in the middle of this air raid scene.

Ask them to open their eyes and share some of these images. Have them write the words 'Air raid' on a piece of paper. Ask them to list the images that came to mind under this first line.

When they have exhausted their ideas ask them to close their eyes again and imagine the bombing suddenly stops and they find they are safe. What would it be like? What can they hear? How would they feel? Get them to open their eyes and list four to six of these images or feelings before repeating the first line 'Air raid'.

Explain to the students that they have just written poetry. Ask them to share some of the poems they have written.

AIR RAID
by Jane S. (10 yrs)

Air Raid,
  screaming,
gunpowder, smoke,
  stumbling, terrified,
   footstep pounding,
  sirens wailing,
   fire, confusion,
    gunshots,
    . bombs hitting the ground,
vibrating ground,
never reach the shelter,
   safe,
   silence,
   shock.

  nervousness,
    people crying
    relief
when will it all end?

*A poem written using brainstormed images from the book 'The Machine-Gunners'*

**Follow-up activities**

Following this lesson collect all poems and make a book of the collected work. Choose several students to illustrate the work. Allow all students to borrow the book for personal reading.

**LESSON 4**

The purpose is to look more closely at the character of Boddser and his conflict with Chas. What do we learn about Boddser and Chas in this chapter?

**Procedure**

Read pp. 60-6 of chapter 6.

While Chas won the fight against Boddser by hitting him on the head with his gas mask, he was criticised by his sister, his mates and his father — 'British boys fight with their fists'. Ask the class to discuss Chas' actions in groups of four to six students. Was he justified? How would you have reacted? What caused the anger that seemed to well up inside Chas?

After discussing the incident with Boddser ask the groups to share experiences they have had of their own 'Boddsers'.

## Follow-up activities

Invite the students to write a newspaper report on one of the events Chas witnessed on the way to his grandparents' home. For example:

- the destruction of Ronnie Boyce's home
- the discovery of the unexploded bomb
- the destruction of Saville Street
- the collapse of the church spire.

Share several real newspaper clippings on overhead and discuss their features. Point out that a newspaper article tells the readers: Who. What. When. Where. Why. Allow students to write the newspaper articles alone or in pairs. Provide time for them to be shared with the whole class.

Missing German Gun Used to Down German Plane

Nicholas (11yrs)

A German plane was shot down yesterday by a missing machine gun believed to be held by teenagers. Teenagers are believed to have a base in an old directly hit house. The gun is believed to have beeen stolen from a German Bomber which was shot down last month.

*A newspaper article written in response to 'The Machine-Gunners'*

## LESSON 5

The major focus is on the complexity of the methods used during the second world war. The novel is filled with the technical terminology of war, all of which was part of the everyday language of the time. An examination of this specialised knowledge is valuable background for the reading of the story.

### Procedure

Read on in chapter 6 to the point when the air raid ends.

Following the reading discuss the details of the air raid. What were *barrage balloons* and what was their purpose? What were *tracers*, *ack ack gunners*, *cordite*, a *Buster*, a *Dornier Do 17*, and a *Junkers 88*?

Research the details of air warfare that dominated the lives of Chas and his friends. Organise a bulk loan of reference books on warfare, WW2 fighters, and the Battle of Britain.

As well, try to find someone in the community who could give a talk on WW2 aerial warfare.

### Follow-up activities

a) You might like to show segments of the video movie *Hope and Glory* (Boorman 1987) which is available from most video outlets. The story is set in a community very similar to that portrayed in the novel and provides wonderful sequences concerning the collection of war souvenirs, air raids, the random nature of death and destruction.

   **Please Note** This movie is **not suitable for showing to students in its entirety**, however, if you view it beforehand and select appropriate segments it will provide valuable background information.

b) Some students might like to conduct their own projects on the methods of war that are discussed in the novel. They might also organise a display of model aeroplanes from WW2.

## LESSON 6

The major purpose is to review the characters introduced so far in the novel. Encourage the students to reflect on their personalities and special qualities.

### Procedure

Read the remainder of chapter 6.

Ask the class to brainstorm the complete list of characters introduced so far in the story. Suggest that each student select one of these characters to complete a 'Missing in Action' poster. Stress that the idea of the poster is to think about the description that might be given for the character if they were to disappear. Encourage them to think carefully about the character and personality of their choice and to complete all parts of the poster in such a way that it is consistent with the novel.

## *Missing Person*

| | |
|---|---|
| Name: | CHAS McGILL |
| Other names: | HAWKE EYE, QUICK FINGERS |
| Description: | SHORT, 'WEEDY' BOY APPROXIMATELY 12 YEARS OF AGE. DARK CLOSELY-CUT HAIR. LAST SEEN WEARING SCHOOL UNIFORM CONSISTING OF GREY SHORTS, BLUE SHIRT, GREY JACKET, BLACK SHOES AND LONG, DARK BLUE SOCKS. |
| Last seen: | ON A BOMB SITE IN MARSTON STREET EARLY ON THE MORNING OF NOVEMBER 23RD, 1940. |
| Unusual habits or features: | IS KNOWN TO BE A KEEN COLLECTOR OF WAR SOUVENIRS. SPENDS HIS TIME WITH A GANG OF YOUTHS CONNECTED WITH THE DISAPPEARANCE OF A GERMAN MACHINE-GUN. |
| Comments: | McGILL MAY HAVE BEEN INJURED DURING RECENT RAIDS OR ALTERNATIVELY COULD SIMPLY BE HIDING TO AVOID THE HOME DEFENCE FORCE OFFICERS WHO ARE ANXIOUS TO INTERVIEW HIM. |
| Contact: | HOME DEFENCE FORCES OFFICE WITH ANY INFORMATION. TELEPHONE GARMOUTH 2056. |

## LESSON 7

The major purpose is to discuss the building of the fortress by Chas and his friends. Why did they build it? Was it just a foolish childish prank? The aim of the discussion is for the students to appreciate how the building of the fortress is tied to the frustrations of the war, the desire to be involved, the hatred of an unknown enemy.

### Procedure

Read chapter 7.

Break the class into small groups to discuss *Fortress Caparetto*. What would it be like to have such a fortress? How would you feel about having completed such a hideout? Why was the fortress so important for the children? Was it just another cubby house?

Ask students to draw the fortress showing its location relative to the town and the sea.

### Follow-up activities

Some students might like to construct a three-dimensional model of the fortress from papier mâché.

### LESSON 8

The major purpose is to give students an opportunity to dramatise sections of the chapter. Dramatisation is an extremely effective way to aid identification with and understanding of characters.

#### Procedure

Read chapter 8.

Following the reading, ask the students to respond to the chapter. If necessary ask a number of open questions like the following:

- Is this how you expected the first use of the machine-gun to turn out?
- How would you have felt after the noise stopped and you gazed up to see the massive hole in the roof?
- What would the German pilot's first thoughts be after parachuting to the ground?

After all students have had an opportunity to respond in general terms to the chapter, break the class into groups of three and ask them to dramatise the section of the text describing the reactions (and squabbling) of Cem, Chas and Audrey. Call upon some of these groups to present their dramatisation to the class.

#### Follow-up activities

Some groups might like to dramatise another section of this chapter. Perhaps some might attempt the section at the end of the chapter where Chas talks with his Dad about the telescope.

### LESSON 9

While this lesson is planned mainly to permit more of the text to be read, sketch to stretch will be used to encourage students to make predictions about the plot and engage more deeply in the reading.

#### Procedure

Read chapters 9 and 10, stopping at the point where the children realise an adult is scrambling down the loophole to get into the fortress. Encourage them to predict who it is and what his/her purpose might be. Suggest to your students that they use sketch to stretch to show who it is and what he/she is going to do.

Allow time for the sharing of the sketches with the class then complete the reading of chapter 9.

### LESSON 10

The major purpose is to encourage the students to view the events of the last few chapters from the German airman's perspective. It is important to examine the fact that Westall is able to show that one of the consequences of war is that the people it places in opposition to one another often share many of the same needs in life. In this way the author is able to show the human side of war.

#### Procedure

Read chapter 11.

Allow time for the students to respond in general terms to the chapter, then focus the discussion on Rudi. What was he thinking? What were his plans? How would you have felt in Rudi's situation? What type of person was he? Were Chas and the others able to see that in many ways he was just like them?

**Follow-up activities**

It may be useful to isolate the German words used in this chapter in order to identify their meaning. For example, *Achtung, Tot, Nein, Ja Gut, Krug, Sturmlampe, Ich hatt einen kameraden, lehrer.* Your students might consult an English-German dictionary or find someone who speaks German. You might invite a German-speaking person to provide several basic German lessons.

## LESSON 11

The focus will be the conflict between Boddser and Chas, and the resolution the events of this chapter bring. What does Boddser learn? An attempt will be made to probe deeply into the conflict between the two boys, its cause and the lessons that come from this last fight.

**Procedure**

Read the first part of chapter 12 describing Chas being followed by a mysterious and clever stranger.

Ask the class to break up into small groups to discuss who it might be, why he/she is following, and what he/she intends to do. Suggest that they record their predictions and provide reasons for their choices.

Read the rest of chapter 12 and all of 13.

Allow time to react to the fight between Chas and Boddser and Clogger and Boddser. What feelings did the fight bring to mind? What memories does the text bring to mind of your own conflicts? Have you had to face bullies in your own life? How did you deal with them?

Break the class up into groups of four to six to discuss the questions: Should Clogger Duncan have beaten Boddser the way he did? What did it mean in the story when it said:

> Boddser was much more sick now. When he looked up, his eyes had changed. He looked as if he understood something he had never understood before...

What did he understand?

Following the discussion bring the class back together to share its views.

## LESSON 12

The major aim is to encourage the students to project themselves into the novel. In particular, it would be useful to have them spend time trying to form images of the scenes, and empathy with the situations and characters.

**Procedure**

Read chapters 14 and 15.

Following the reading ask the class to consider how they might feel if an invasion of their country was imminent. Get them to imagine the fears they would face at the prospect of a cruel enemy marching down the main street of their town with bayonets drawn.

<u>Journal Entry for</u>
<u>Mrs McGill</u>

Blast the Germans! First the bombs now this. Never thought I'd see the day they'd set foot on mother England. I can't see how I'll sleep tonight – I now what them thieving killers will do. But not before I take a couple with me. I shoot em, I'll, run em through with the carvin knife, they'll not take me alive.

*A journal entry for the character Mrs McGill in 'The Machine-Gunners'*

Ask the class to close their eyes and imagine the fears they might have. Ask each student to list the 'five things I would fear most'. Share these responses as a group, perhaps recording them on the board or on overhead. Once they have been shared encourage students to use these fears as the basis for a non-rhyming poem titled 'Invasion'.

**Follow-up activities**

Some students might like to write a journal entry for one of the characters in this chapter describing how they saw the events of the night and the threat of the German invasion. Share a journal entry with them and discuss the features of this form of writing, particularly its personal nature.

## LESSON 13

The major focus is the hysteria that surrounded the threat of an invasion. The purpose of class discussions will be to help students appreciate the pressures that Chas, his friends and their families had to face each day. What impact must this have had on their lives?

**Procedure**

Read chapters 16 and 17.

Allow time for general responses to these chapters then focus on the news that the invasion had not begun. How would the people have felt? Imagine what it would be like to live with the constant threat of invasion.

Discuss the fact that many people today live with the threat of invasion and others have already experienced invasion. Identify some of the world's trouble spots where foreign powers are occupying territories that are not their own. Locate these places on a map and encourage students to research the background to these conflicts.

**Follow-up activities**

Some students might like to write a newspaper account of the air raid detailing the trail of destruction, and the mistaken fears of the townspeople that the raid was a full German invasion.

## LESSON 14

The purpose is to complete the reading of the story and draw together some of the major themes in it. In particular, an effort will be made to examine the impact of war on the children and the 'two worlds' in which they were forced to live. How was the perspective of these children different to their parents? Why? How well did the parents understand the children (and vice versa)?

**Procedure**

Read chapter 18.

Allow time for the students to indicate how they feel about the ending to this story. Is it how they expected it to end? If not, how did they expect it to end?

Focus the discussion on the final confrontation with their parents and the police. What did the narrator mean by:

> The world had two faces. Which was the true one? The world of the long night of waiting, of Stukas and Panzers, stormtroopers and death? Or the world of day, of punishments, hidings and magistrate's court?

Why is this thought so important to the whole novel? What does it say about the reality of war for these children?

Finish the lesson by discussing the consequences of the decisions made about each of the children at the end of the chapter. What effect would these decisions have on the children? Are they the decisions they would have made?

**Follow-up activities**

a) As part of the above discussions or as an additional sharing time ask the class to consider the generation gap between these children and their parents. How well did the parents understand them and the impact of the war on their lives? Which adult seemed to understand the children best? Why?

b) Introduce your students to the Westall novel which followed *The Machine-Gunners* — *Fathom Five* (1979). This novel is set two years later and concerns Chas McGill's investigations of people whom he suspects of spying for the Germans.

CHAPTER SIXTEEN                                    # Sounder

**Literature:**     *Sounder*, William H. Armstrong
**Suggested Level:**   Grades five to eight

## SYNOPSIS

*Sounder* (1969) is a moving novel about a black sharecropping family living in the southern part of the United States. The time period in which the story is set is not given in the novel, but it is probably the 1920s to 1930s. The story tells of the hardship and injustice faced by a black woman, her teenage son, and three small children after their husband and father is taken off to gaol. The father is arrested early in the story for stealing a ham to feed his family. Sounder, the family's dog is shot as the father is taken away.

However, the animal survives and becomes a companion to the boy as he faces the loss of his father with great courage and determination. Armstrong paints a picture of the hardship endured by black Americans early in this century. In doing so he also provides an insight into the way relationships are strengthened, and character is moulded, as people face repression and injustice.

## PROGRAM FOCUS

While there are many things on which one could focus when studying this book, I would encourage my students to:
a) Focus on the way the author creates a strong sense of setting and context.
b) Discuss the way the author shows the strength of relationships between characters within the story.
c) Examine the themes of cruelty (which grows out of racism), fear, loneliness, isolation and powerlessness.

## POSSIBLE LESSONS

### LESSON 1

Before commencing the reading of the story read the author's note to the class. This short foreword gives the reader an insight into the context from which this story emerged. In stressing that *Sounder* was based on a tale told to him as a child by a wise old black, Armstrong provides an important link between the story as written, and the historical reality of repression and cruelty faced by black Americans.

### Procedure

After reading this short introduction ask the class a number of questions:

- Why has Armstrong written this note to us?
- Why has storytelling been so important through the ages?
- Can you ever remember being *told* (as distinct from read) stories?
- Who told you the stories?
- What type of stories were they?
- Where were you when the stories were told?
- Where did the storyteller get his/her story?

After this initial discussion read the first part of chapter 1 (pp. 9-17).

Once you've finished this section conclude the lesson without further discussion, unless students spontaneously ask questions or respond in some way.

### LESSON 2

In this lesson the reading of chapter 1 would be completed, and an attempt made to encourage the class to visualise the setting. This would involve discussion of the physical hardship faced by the family, balanced always by the strength and depth of the emotional bonds between family members.

### Procedure

Begin by reading the rest of chapter 1.

At the conclusion of the lesson ask the students to comment on the quality of life that the family had. What was life like for this family?

Break the class into groups of four to six to examine this question. To make it more personal ask the groups to consider what they think would be the hardest thing to endure themselves. Nominate leaders for each group and ask them to list all the points made. After approximately fifteen minutes ask the groups to report back to the whole class.

After this sharing re-read the section of the chapter that relates how the boy described the oak slab, the times when the slab had ham on it before, and the experience of eating the ham and hot 'biscuits'.

Ask the students to close their eyes and picture the scene as it is read. Ask them to imagine how they might feel if they were the boy. Sometime during the discussion you may need to explain that a 'biscuit' looks like a scone, but is not sweet and is normally eaten as part of a meal instead of bread.

Finish the lesson by asking the students to try to recall special times and places that have given them the same feeling of 'warmth' the boy must have experienced. Ask them to share these with the class.

### LESSON 3

This lesson would again focus on setting. However, as an extension it might well consider the social context in which the story is set. As a consequence of their discussions students might contrast the treatment of blacks in the time period of the novel, with the treatment of black Americans and Australians today.

*One student's response to the invitation to use sketch to stretch for 'Sounder'*

### Procedure

Start the lesson by reading chapter 2.

At the conclusion of the reading ask the students to think about Sounder's plight. Is he alive, or dead? Will he be found? Where might he be? Don't provide an opportunity for the students to discuss these questions at this stage.

Instead, ask them to close their eyes and consider the questions attempting to visualise Sounder's situation. After approximately two to three minutes ask the students to sketch the image they have in mind.

This simple technique is designed to encourage students to use drawing to represent the meanings they create as they read. An example of a sketch that one student produced as part of this lesson appears here.

### Follow-up activities

If some students are sufficiently motivated, you might encourage them to draw a map of the cabin and the surrounding countryside.

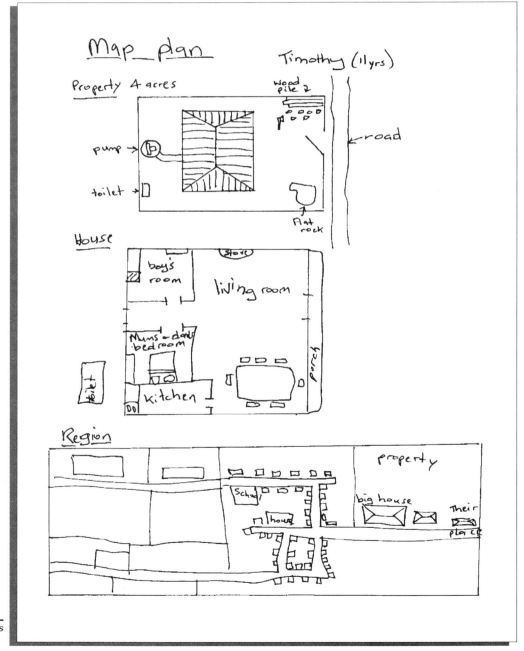

*A map of Sounder's home territory*

As a follow-up (or as an alternative to the sketch to stretch activity) you might ask your students to write a newspaper account of the father's crime and arrest. Discuss with the class how this article might have been presented in a newspaper owned and run by white people. What aspects of the crime would have been accentuated? How accurately would it have been reported?

As a natural follow-up some students might want to discuss the issue of bias in the press of today. This could be done in small groups and might lead to the examination of selected articles, identical stories reported in different newspapers, and so on.

## LESSON 4

This lesson is concerned primarily with the emotional suffering that the man's imprisonment would have caused to the family. In particular, the effect on the mother would be discussed.

### Procedure

Start by reading chapter 3 right through without interruption. After reading the chapter allow students to offer general responses. Following a brief discussion re-read the section where the mother heads off alone to return the stolen goods.

> As his mother stepped off the porch and started for the road she began to hum softly to herself. It was a song the boy had heard her sing many nights in the cabin:
>
> *You gotta walk that lonesome valley,*
> *You gotta walk it by yourself,*
> *Ain't nobody else gonna walk it for you.*
>
> The boy wanted to run after her...
>
> And Sounder too, settin' on his haunches, would speak to the moon in ghost-stirrin' tones of lonesome dog-talk.

After reading this section break the class into groups of four to six students to discuss the following questions:

- What has the mother gone to do?
- What must she have been thinking as she walked off?
- What might the boy have been thinking? What might be the significance of his recollections of his father at this time?

### *Sample responses to the question: What has the mother gone to do?*

She has gone to find the father and has hidden the dog in her sack to sell. (Sarah, age 9)

She has gone to town to sell the kurnells to get the bail for her husband. (Andrew, age 10)

I think the mother is going to town to trade the kurnells for some sow-belly and potatoes. (Simon, age 10)

I think the mother has gone to give the kurnells and meat to pay back for the ham they stole and ate. (Marc, age 10)

What a catostrapie! My husband has been arrested for stealing some meat. Our family was desparate thaugh and he couldn't help it. The need for food was killing us all. Even worse the deputies shot Sounder and the boy is boking for him. I took Sounder some meat, and the kernels to town. I hope to bail out my husband and B heal Sounder. Although I'm afraid nuts can't do all that!

Fiona (9 yrs)

*A journal entry written for the mother in 'Sounder'*

Appoint a group leader and ask him/her to write down all of the group's responses. These should eventually be shared with the whole class.

**Follow-up activities**

As a follow-up perhaps invite your students to complete one of the following:

a) Prepare a diary or journal entry for the mother written at the end of the day after her journey into town with the stolen goods. Alternatively, this could be done for the boy. Remind the students that it should be written in the first person with self as audience. Encourage them to describe their feelings.

b) Ask your students to think about a time when they were desperate to find something. Have them talk to a partner about it before describing the time and the situation.

c) Have students in pairs consider the conversation that might have occurred between the mother and the rich white family as she returns the stolen goods. Encourage your students to record the conversation and present it as a dramatic presentation for the class.

## LESSON 5

The focus of this lesson is on the hardship and cruelty faced by the black family. It is important to allow students to compare their experiences of cruelty with those portrayed in the novel.

### Procedure

Begin by reading chapter 4 without comment. This chapter describes the boy's trip to the gaol to see his father and to deliver the cake.

After the reading ask the students to share their reactions to the characters and incidents. What were their feelings towards the gaoler? How did they feel about the boy's experience?

After this discussion re-read the section which describes the gaol and the boy's encounter with the man who crushes the cake, and which finishes with the boy feeling hatred for the deputy. Break the class into groups of four to six and ask them to share experiences that they have had of cruelty. What was it like? How did they deal with it? What feelings did they have towards the person who was being cruel? Once the groups have shared their experiences you might like to share as a class.

### Follow-up activities

Encourage students to think of other books in which cruelty occurs. Ask them to share the books they recall in the whole class group.

### LESSON 6

This is simply a reading session. Chapter 5 tells of Sounder's return and is an important turning point in the story. Read it to the class without expecting a response. However, if students want to share thoughts or ask questions at the end of the chapter allow them to do so.

### LESSON 7

The emphasis in this lesson is on the way in which the story shows the effects of loneliness and fear upon people. As well, it would be useful to encourage students to relate these same feelings to their own lives.

### Procedure

Begin by reading chapter 6.

Word banks concerning 'Fear' and 'Loneliness' created in response to 'Sounder'

This chapter, which follows Sounder's return, is a picture of despair, hopelessness and loneliness. Encourage the students to consider why the family seem so discouraged in this chapter. Why are their spirits nearing breaking point?

As well, encourage them to predict what might occur later in the story. Would the boy's father return? Has all hope gone? Would they give up?

After discussing the chapter invite the class to write a poem titled 'Loneliness', or alternatively 'Fear'. Before writing the poem ask the class to think of words that express fear or loneliness. Ask all students to compile their own lists in pairs.

Allow approximately five minutes for your students to brainstorm words for fear or loneliness then present a specific poetic form for them to use as a model when writing their own. A variety of forms could be used, but a loose form of cinquain often works well. This poem would take the following form:

### Loneliness (or Fear)

. . . . . . . . . . . Two words describing their feelings.

. . . . . . . . . . . Three words describing an action related to their feeling of fear or loneliness.

. . . . . . . . . . . Two words about their secret hopes in the face of this fear or loneliness.

. . . . . . . . . . . A synonym for the title and first line.

The following are examples of poems written by grade five students in response to this activity:

Fear

Fear,
Shivering, Scared,
Running away, cold,
Afraid of the dark,
Coward.

By Marc + Sam (Age 10)

Lonliness

Lonliness
no friends
very very Scared
No-one to play with
Bored

*Poems on 'Fear' and 'Loneliness' using word banks generated from 'Sounder'*

## LESSON 8

The aim is to complete the reading of the story and allow the students to discuss how Armstrong resolves the tension he has built up.

### Procedure

Begin by reading the first two paragraphs of chapter 7 which reveal to the reader that there has been a terrible dynamite blast at a quarry where the boy's father has been kept prisoner. Encourage the students to predict what might have happened to the father as a result of the blast. How would the mother and the boy feel at this stage? What might be some of their fears?

Complete the reading of the rest of chapter 7 and all of chapter 8 without further comment. At the end of the reading, break the class into groups of four to six to share their reactions to the story's ending.

Meet again as a class and ask the students to compare the parts of the novel which have had the greatest impact upon them.

### Follow-up activities

After the above general discussion you might ask your students to consider the character that they felt they associated most closely with during the reading. Have them share their answers and ask them to reflect on the reasons for the diversity of responses.

## LESSON 9

This lesson is optional and would only be attempted with mature readers. Its focus is racism.

### Procedure

Ask the class to brainstorm the ways in which the racism of the period in which the novel was set has been realised in the lives of the main characters. Break the class into groups of four to six and ask leaders to record all responses.

**Note** It may be necessary to point out some of the more subtle forms of racism, e.g. the fact that when the father is arrested he is called 'boy'.

After the group has shared these responses encourage them to discuss the extent to which these same examples of racism are shown in today's society.

### Follow-up activities

A possible extension of the discussions is to point out to the class that the author has been accused of being racist himself. Point out that only the dog has a name in the story. Critics have suggested that in doing this Armstrong is guilty of doing exactly what whites did in the Deep South, they refused to call black people by their names. This denies their equality and dehumanises them. However, Armstrong has been defended by some who claim that he may have left the main characters without names simply to give them a universal appeal. Ask the class to consider their views on this contentious issue.

CHAPTER SEVENTEEN | # Playing Beatie Bow

**Literature:** *Playing Beatie Bow* (1984), Ruth Park
**Suggested Level:** Grades six to eight

## SYNOPSIS

This piece of historical fiction concerns a 14-year-old girl (Abigail Kirk) living in a luxury apartment block in The Rocks area of Sydney. Abigail notices a strange little girl hiding in the shadows of the apartment playground while children are playing a game called 'Beatie Bow'. She tries to speak to her, and follows her as she runs away. As she climbs a set of stairs and runs into a street she suddenly finds herself in a strange place, The Rocks as it was in 1873. Abigail becomes involved with a strange family, falls in love with Judah (a young sailor), and learns that life in Victorian Sydney was much more difficult and frightening than she could ever imagine.

## PROGRAM FOCUS

There are many aspects of this text worthy of attention — many will arise incidentally as it is read and discussed. However, a number of major concerns will be:
a) The pivotal relationship between Judah and Abigail and its effect upon Abigail's 'coming of age'.
b) The conflict between Abigail and her parents and her resolution of these conflicts.
c) The setting in which the story takes place and the insights into the history of Sydney that it gives, particularly the life-style of the times.

## POSSIBLE LESSONS

### LESSON 1

The major purpose is to introduce the novel and discuss the central character — Abigail Kirk. It is important to consider the relationship between Abigail and her parents, and the impact that their separation has on her.

## Procedure

Read chapter 1 without comment.

At the end of the chapter ask the class for their opinions of Abigail. What is she like? Why did she change her name? What is at the root of Abigail's actions? It is important that the class at least consider the interpretation that Abigail's actions are connected with her parents' separation.

Ask the class also to comment on the game Beatie Bow. Have they ever seen a game like this? Where might it have come from? Can they recall other games which they have played regularly during their childhoods involving chants or rhymes?

## Follow-up activities

Some students might like to conduct their own research on playground games involving rituals or chants. Compile a list and description of the games. They might also attempt to trace the origin of each.

## LESSON 2

The major purpose is to again examine the character of Abigail and her relationship with her mother. As well, sketch to stretch will be used to help students engage more fully in the plot.

## Procedure

Begin reading chapter 2 stopping at the point where Abigail and her mother stop arguing and Abigail finally goes off to bed. Discuss Abigail's and her mother's actions. Was Abigail justified to take the stand she took? Did she have any right to be angry? What about her mother, was she being naive?

Continue reading the chapter, stopping at the point where Abigail feels drawn to hold out her hand to the little girl and say, 'Oh, Mudda, what's that, what can it be?'

Ask your students to predict what might be going to occur. Get them to close their eyes and try to imagine the scene. Encourage them to use sketch to stretch to show what they think will occur.

After the sketches have been shared in small groups of four to six students, read the rest of the chapter without comment. At the end of the reading ask the students to comment on what has happened. Were the predictions accurate? What has happened to Abigail Kirk?

*One response to the invitation to use sketch to stretch for 'Playing Beatie Bow'*

## LESSON 3

The major focus is the setting and the historical period in which the story is set. What are the differences between Sydney today and Sydney in 1873? What would be the most striking differences for someone like Abigail thrust into a time that was not her own?

### Procedure

Read chapter 3.

In this chapter we read how Abigail finally comes face to face with the realisation that she is now living in the year 1873. What would she be thinking and feeling at this stage? What would she notice that is different? What might be the most striking changes that she becomes aware of in: The Rocks, Sydney generally, and life in this period?

Break the class into groups of four to six students to consider these questions. Select a leader to act as recorder who is willing to report back the group's views to the class.

Using a modern map of The Rocks try to establish where Abigail is living and from where she has come. Prepare a large map labelling all the prominent landmarks mentioned in the story. Display the map for reference during the rest of the story. Encourage the class to make additions as the story proceeds. Alternatively, allow groups to prepare their own maps for display and ready reference.

### Follow-up activities

Some students might want to prepare their own sketch plan of the Bow house and shop. Perhaps this could include a front elevation as well as internal floor plans and illustrative sketches of parts of the house and furnishings.

A constant source of interest throughout the novel is the language that is used. Encourage the students to look closely at the language. Research the origin and meaning of specific words, *bairnie*, *hot pig*, *dunna ken*.

## LESSON 4

The purpose is to continue the story and examine further the historical setting. An examination of the lifestyle of this era is important for a full appreciation of the story. As well, students will be encouraged to consider 'The Gift' and its relationship to the story plot. What is this all about? Why is it important to the story?

### Procedure

Read chapter 4 without interruption.

After the reading encourage students to list the elements of lifestyle that Abigail would have found different, looking especially at clothing, health and standard of living. Ask the students to consider the things that they would have found hardest about life in this period. Perhaps prepare a class list of 'Things I Would Hate'.

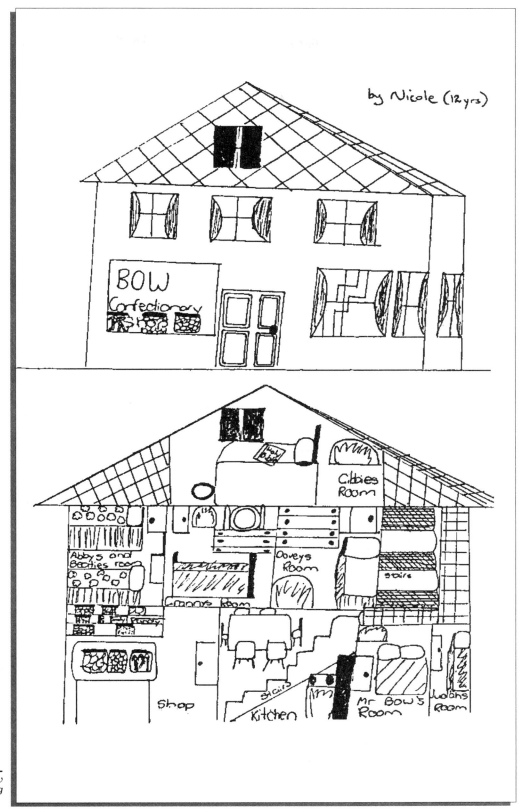

*A sketch of the Bow house in 'Playing Beatie Bow'*

### *Things I Would Hate...*

I would hate...
Using a pot to go to the toilet,
Not being able to shower,
Living with the threat of death from simple
diseases,
Wearing all those clothes,
Being afraid to walk the streets,
Putting up with crazy Mr Bow,
The brat upstairs,
Not being able to get back home,
Not having TV,
Just about everything.

Ask the class to think about the mention of 'The Stranger', 'The Gift' and 'Elfland' in this chapter. What is this all about?

#### Follow-up activities
Some students might like to research the diseases of Victorian times. Encourage them to consider infant mortality, the standard of medical care for the poor, the death rate from specific common diseases etc.

## LESSON 5

The major focus is the culture of the Victorian era in which the story is set. The customs and religious conviction of the people and the way this is interwoven with their lives.

#### Procedure
Read chapter 5.

a) It is important for students to consider the customs of the time reflected in this novel. For example, there was a great preoccupation with death in the Victorian era, related in part to the mortality rate from common diseases. Gibbie's obsession with his death in the early pages of this chapter provides an insight into the morbidity of Victorian people. As a class discuss this cultural preoccupation as well as the likely roots of this tendency. As well, consider other unusual customs that are evident in the Bow family.

b) As a class discuss the religious influences of this time. It is important to discuss the fact that life was often influenced strongly by a faith rooted in obedience to God's law. Christian faith frequently stressed God's judgement and wrath upon those who sinned. This is seen clearly in the comments of the Bow family. For example:

"It's evil to gamble," said Gibbie shocked.

"You blasphemed," he gasped.

"You ought to be ashamed, telling me such lees. You'll go to hell for it, and be toasted on a pitchfork!" (said Beatie).

## LESSON 6

The major focus is once again the lifestyle of the era. However, this time concentrate on the inequalities between the rich and the poor. An associated interest in the lesson is the exploitation of the poor as evidenced in the kidnapping of young men and women into various types of slavery.

### Procedure

Read chapter 6.

In groups of four to six encourage the students to discuss the class inequalities that existed at this time. Ask the groups to record the differences for sharing with the class. As well, ask them to consider the things Beatie would normally have been denied because her family were poor. When the class shares these points ensure that the role of 'Ragged Schools' is discussed fully. If possible, obtain accurate historical information to share with your pupils.

> Differences between Ragged Schools and rich people's schools.
>
> Better teachers in proper schools.
> Bigger classes in ragged schools.
> Poorer equipment in ragged schools.
> In the proper school they would've taught kids more about manners.
> The kids were not as clever in the ragged schools.
> The subjects taught in ragged school were not as good.
> Kids in ragged schools were not as confident.
>
> Marie (12 yrs)

*One child's brainstormed list of inequalities shown in everyday life in 'Playing Beatie Bow'*

Re-read the section of the chapter dealing with Abigail's kidnapping. Break the class into groups of four to six to discuss how Abigail must have felt. Encourage them to predict what might happen to Abigail. Will she escape? How will she do it?

### Follow-up activities

Some students might like to research the type of education offered to children in the Victorian era. If the class's own school was functioning in 1873 ask them to research the form of education offered to children at this time.

## LESSON 7

The major purpose is to discuss the 'Prophecy', 'The Gift' and 'The Stranger'. Each of these is of critical importance to Abigail's journey back in time. What do they mean? How are they of importance?

### Procedure

Read chapter 7.

It is in this chapter that the nature of 'The Gift', the role of 'The Stranger' and the 'Prophecy' become clearer. How was Abigail connected with the Bows and Taliskers, what was the part she was to play? What was the 'Prophecy'? Who was to die?

### Follow-up activities

Some students might like to consider writing a journal entry for Abigail dealing either with her terrible experience in the 'Suez canal' or her discoveries and thoughts about the 'Prophecy'.

## LESSON 8

The purpose is to continue the discussion of the 'Prophecy' begun in the last lesson. Of special importance in this chapter is the part played by the dress that Abigail wore as she stumbled into The Rocks of 1873. Why is this important? How will it help Abigail to return?

### Procedure

Read part of chapter 8 stopping at the point just before Granny reveals the whereabouts of the dress.

One of the major concerns in this chapter is Abigail's return to her own time. The dress has an important part to play in this. Break the class into groups of four to six and ask them to discuss the importance of the dress. Why did she need it? Where might it be? Suggest that they use sketch to stretch to show where they think it is hidden.

Read the rest of the chapter and allow time for responses and discussion at the end of the lesson.

### Follow-up activities

Discuss with your students the fact that 'time slip' novels frequently have an object or place which has great importance to the passage through time. For example, in Tom's Midnight Garden (Pearce 1986) we have an old clock and a pair of rusting ice skates which assume importance. Ask the class to think of other examples and discuss the reasons that authors might use them.

## LESSON 9

The major focus in this lesson is the relationship between Abigail and Judah. Judah is of central importance in the total plot for this story. It is important to encourage the class to discuss fully the relationship that developed between them and the effect that this had on Abigail.

**Note** If using this book with younger children (e.g. grade six) you need to handle this very sensitively. In many ways it has less significance for children who have not yet entered puberty.

### Procedure

Read chapter 9.

In this chapter the growing relationship between Abigail and Judah is given prominence. Is Abigail in love with Judah? Is Judah in love with her? What is she learning about herself as she realises she feels differently towards him than any other boy she has known before? How is this linked to the description of her which we read right at the beginning of the book:

> Now she was fourteen and, as with many other girls of her age, her inside did not match her outside at all. The outside was nothing to beat drums about...Outside, she was composed, independent, not very much liked...The girls said she was unreal...She felt a hundred years older and wiser than this love-mad rabble in her class (pp. 3-4).

As a class discuss these questions then suggest that students prepare a diary entry for Abigail that might have been written the night after she went cockling with Judah. What might she have written? How would she have felt? Would there have been confusion in her mind?

### Follow-up activities

As a class you might attempt to locate Cockle Bay on a map. Where is Cockle Bay today? What is it used for?

Students might also discuss the practice of cockling. What are cockles? What were they used for in 1873? Do people still go cockling now? Why do they collect them?

## LESSON 10

In this chapter we are faced with the realisation that Judah and Abigail are not meant for each other. But the relationship with Judah has changed Abigail. On her return to her own time her mother clearly notices the difference. This coming of age, of new maturity and insight, is of critical importance. The major focus in this lesson will be a discussion of this theme.

### Procedure

Read chapter 10 without comment.

Wednesday, September 12th, 1873

Today I went cockling down at Cockle Cove with Beatie and Judah. Granny said that Judah would pick between Dovey and me so I was really nervous. I also had a terrible feeling that today was going to be my last day here. Judah and I had a wonderful day, we ran around over the rocks and of course went cockling. We went out in the boat. I started crying because I thought today was my last day here, then suddenly he kissed me – a proper kiss! He was really ashamed of himself but I told him how much I loved him. Beatie saw us kissing and had a terrible tantrum. I don't really blame her since Judah has to marry Dovey because he made her lame. Judah managed to get Beatie into the boat, but could not talk any sense into her. She was determined to tell Dovey. I felt terrible!

But when we got back to the house there was another disaster waiting for us. Mr Bow was drunk again and had set the house on fire. Dovey had been trapped inside after she had remembered the trunk with my dress inside. We pushed it out the window onto the street below. Then Dovey suddenly remembered Gibbie so I climbed up the stairs to get him. He was reluctant to come and I had to pull him out the window. The chinamen from the laundry next door held their baskets out for us to jump into. Gibbie wouldn't jump so I had to practically push him out the window. Then I saw Judah. He ran up to Dovey and hugged and kissed her. Granny was right he had decided who he loved today. I had a feeling that I'm going to leave tomorrow.

A diary entry for Abigail from the book 'Playing Beatie Bow'

At the conclusion of the chapter ask the class to comment on Abigail's final statement: 'Good-bye, Judah, good-bye,' she said.

What had Abigail finally realised?

Read chapter 11 without comment.

At the end of the chapter break the class into groups of three to five to discuss the chapter. Suggest to the groups that they offer general responses first — How do you feel after reading this chapter? Are you satisfied with the way things have worked out? Try to imagine how Abigail might have felt.

After the groups have had sufficient time to respond ask them to look specifically at the dream Abigail had about Judah at sea (p. 170). What might this have meant? What is the significance of the fact that Abigail's mother notices that she is different? Is she different? In what ways? What is it that her mother notices? What has changed? Why does Abigail suddenly have a change of attitude?

After the groups have had sufficient time to discuss these questions bring them together to share their ideas.

## LESSON 11

The purpose of this lesson is primarily to conclude the novel and to encourage the class to respond to it as a whole.

### Procedure

Read chapter 12 without comment.

As a class discuss the events of the chapter. Were they unexpected? Did anyone realise it was Judah all along who was going to die?

Read chapter 13.

Allow time for responses of a general nature. How do they feel about the ending? Could it have ended another way? After this discussion turn the students' attention to the 'Prophecy' and the events that we have now pieced together. Exactly what has happened to the Bows and Talliskers?

Who is this young man that enters Abigail's life? Perhaps prepare a diary entry that Abigail might have written that night after meeting Robert Bow. What would her thoughts and feelings be? How would she reconcile the pieces of the Bow story with the arrival of Robert? What would she be thinking about her future?

### Follow-up activities

In small groups ask your students to prepare a family tree for the Bows and Talliskers. Use the text to piece together the web of relationships that have now been revealed.

# CHAPTER EIGHTEEN

# The Last Word

My major hope in writing this book was that it might help teachers to enthuse their students about the endless possibilities of literature. It is hoped that after reading the previous seventeen chapters you will never again teach reading as a school subject that fills neat slots in your teaching program. My hope is that your teaching will be interrupted by the unexpected sharing of favourite books when least expected, by spontaneous responses to individual or group reading, and by frequent changes of plans as one book 'flops', and another captures everyone's imagination. Well-planned lessons will be scrapped because no-one cares less whether Charlotte might have kept a journal, nor how Templeton might look on a police mugsheet. And informal talk about books will regularly punctuate the day. In short, the degree to which you have been successful in implementing the ideas shared in this book, will probably be inversely related to the 'orderliness' with which literature is used in your classrooms.

If you have succeeded in creating a community of readers and writers, then the common ground which binds the members of this group together will have been expanded greatly by books. Your students will have discovered that literature presents them with endless possibilities and limitless worlds waiting to be explored and experienced for the first time.

I hope that your classrooms will be filled with students who value books and who do more than just look at them on the library shelves. As I stated in chapter 1, one of the realities of readers in western schools in the 1980s and 90s is that most students can read, but they fail to do so except for utilitarian and school-related purposes. Charlotte Huck (1973, p.203) has something insightful to say about this phenomenon:

> If we teach a child to read yet develop not the taste for reading all our teaching is for naught. We shall have produced a nation of illiterate literates — those who know how to read but do not read.

Storytelling is as old as human history itself. People have always communicated and learnt primarily through narrative. Hardy (1978, p.13) suggests that all constructs of reality are stories, and narrative is the most effective way people make sense of their world:

We dream in narrative, day-dream in narrative, remember, anticipate, hope, despair, believe, doubt, plan, revise, criticise, construct, gossip, learn, hate, love by narrative...we make up stories about ourselves and others, about the personal as well as the social past and future.

In a sense, life is illogical and meaningless unless we use narrative to give it shape and form. The hope of this book is that the ideas it presents will transform classrooms from clinics for the study of written language into active communities of language users, for whom narrative has a transforming effect. Places where people are bound together by a common commitment and excitement about the power of story.

# Bibliography

Allington, R. L. 'If they don't read much, how they ever gonna be good?' *Journal of Reading*, 21, 1, 1977.

Allington, R. L. 'Teacher interruption behaviours during primary grade oral reading'. *Journal of Educational Psychology*, 72, 1980.

Allington, R. L. 'The reading instruction provided readers of differing reading abilities'. *Elementary School Journal*, 83, 1983.

Alpert, J. 'Teacher behaviour across ability groups'. *Journal of Educational Psychology*, 66, 1974

Atwell, N. 'Writing and reading literature from the inside out'. *Language Arts*, 61, 3, 1984.

Atwell, N. *In the Middle: Writing, Reading, and Learning with Adolescents*, Portsmouth, N.H.: Boynton/Cook, 1987.

Bakhtin, M. *Problems of Dostoevsky's Poetics* (1929), trans. R. W. Rotsel. Ann Arbor, Mich.: Ardis Publications, 1973.

Barthes, R. *The Pleasure of the Text*. New York: Hill & Wang, 1975.

Bettelheim, B. *The Uses of Enchantment: The Meaning and Importance of Fairy Tales*. New York: Knopf, 1976.

Bleich, D. *Subjective Criticism*. Baltimore, Md.: The Johns Hopkins University Press, 1978.

Bloome, D. 'Reading as a social process'. *Language Arts*, 62, 2, 1985.

Bruner, J. *Actual Minds, Possible Worlds*. Harvard University Press. Cambridge Mass., 1986.

Cairney, T. H. *Balancing the Basics: A Handbook for Teachers of Reading, K-8*. Portsmouth, N.H.: Heinemann, 1985a.

Cairney, T. H. *Users, not consumers of language: One class takes control of its own learning* in proceedings of the 11th Australian Reading Association Conference, Brisbane, 4-7 July, 1985b.

Cairney, T. H. *Helping Children to Make Meaning*. Wagga Wagga: Riverina Literacy Centre, 1986.

Cairney, T. H. 'The social foundations of literacy'. *Australian Journal of Reading*, 10, 2, 1987a.

Cairney, T. H. 'Changing children's attitudes towards learning: From consumers to users of language' in J. Hancock & B. Comber, eds. *Independent Learners*. Sydney: Methuen, 1987b.

Cairney, T. H. 'Character mugsheets'. *The Reading Teacher*, 41, 3, 1987c.

Cairney, T. H. *The influence of intertextuality upon the reading and writing of children aged 6-12 years*. Final report of ARC funded project, 1987d.

Cairney, T. H. 'Perceptions of basal readers: What children think'. *The Reading Teacher*, 41, 4, 1988a.

Cairney, T. H. 'Teaching reading comprehension: The development of critical and creative readers'. *Australian Journal of Reading*, 11, 3, 1988b.

Cairney, T. H. *The influence of intertextuality upon the reading and writing of children aged 6-12 years*. Paper presented at 12th World Reading Congress, Gold Coast, 5-8 July, 1988c.

Cairney, T. H. & Langbien, S. 'Building communities of readers and writers'. *The Reading Teacher*, 42, 8, 1989.

Clay, M. *Reading: The Patterning of Complex Behaviour*, 1972. Second edition available from Portsmouth, N.H.: Heinemann, 1979.

Corcoran, B. & Evans, E., eds. *Readers, Texts, Teachers*. Portsmouth, N.H.: Boynton/Cook, 1987.

Early, M. J. 'Stages of growth in literary appreciation'. *English Journal*, 49, 1960.

Eder, D. 'Ability grouping as a self-fulfilling prophecy'. *Sociology of Education*, 54, 1981.

Fox, G. 'Dark watchers: Young readers and their fiction'. *English Education*, 13, 1, 1979.

Freire, P. & Macedo, D. *Literacy: Reading the Word and the World*. South Hadley, Mass.: Bergin & Garvey, 1987.

Gambrell, L. B., Wilson, R. M. & Gantt, W. N. 'An analysis of task attending behaviours of good and poor readers' in R. M. Wilson *Diagnostic and Remedial Reading*. Columbus, Ohio: Charles E. Merrill, 1981.

Groff, P. 'A survey of basal reading group practices'. *Reading Teacher*, 15, 1962.

Haas Dyson, A. 'Writing and the social lives of children'. *Language Arts*, 62, 6, 1985.

Halliday, M. A. K. *Learning How to Mean*. New York: Elsevier North-Holland, 1975.

Halliday, M. A. K. *Language as Social Semiotic*. London: Edward Arnold, 1978.

Hardy, B. 'Narrative as a primary act of the mind' in M. Meek, A. Warlow & G. Barton, eds. *The Cool Web: The Pattern of Children's Reading*. New York: Atheneum, 1978.

Heath, S. B. *Ways with Words: Language, Life, and Work in Communities and Classrooms*. New York: Cambridge University Press, 1983.

Hoffman, J., O'Neal, S., Kastler, L., Clements, R., Segel, K. & Nash, M. 'Guided oral reading and miscue focused verbal feedback in second-grade classrooms'. *Reading Research Quarterly*, 19, 1984.

Holdaway, D. *Independence in Reading*, 1972. Second edition, 1980, available in U.S. from Portsmouth, N.H.: Heinemann.

Huck, C. S. 'Strategies for improving interest and appreciation in literature' in P. G. Burns & L. M Schell, eds. *Elementary School Language Arts*. Chicago: Rand McNally, 1973.

Hutchings, M. 'What teachers are demonstrating' in J. Newman, ed. *Whole Language: Theory in Use*. Portsmouth, N.H.: Heinemann, 1985.

Iser, W. *The Act of Reading: A Theory of Aesthetic Response*. Baltimore, Md.: The Johns Hopkins University Press, 1978.

Johnson, T. & Louis, D. *Literacy Through Literature*. Porthsmouth, N.H.: Heinemann, 1985.

Keifer, B. 'The responses of children in a combination first/second grade classroom to picture books in a variety of artistic styles'. *Journal of Research and Development in Education*, vol. 16, 1983.

Kuhn, T. S. *The Structure of Scientific Revolutions*, second edition. Chicago: Chicago University Press, 1970.

McVitty, W. 'Send their imaginations soaring'. *Weekend Australian,* March 29-30, 1986.

Meek, M. See Spencer, M. Meek.

Pflum, S., Pascarella, E., Boskwick, W. & Awer, C. 'The influence of pupil behaviours and pupil status factors on teacher behaviours during oral reading lessons'. *Journal of Education Research,* 74, 1980.

Rist, R. 'Student social class and teacher expectations'. *Harvard Educational Review*, 40, 1970.

Rosenblatt, L. *The Reader, the Text, the Poem*. Carbondale, Ill.: Southern Illinois University Press, 1978.

Saxby, M. 'The gift of wings: the value of literature to children' in M. Saxby & G. Winch, eds. *Give Them Wings: The Experience of Children's Literature*. Melbourne: Macmillan, 1987.

Smith, F. *Understanding Reading*. New York: Holt, Rinehart & Winston, 1978.

Smith, F. *Joining the Literacy Club*. Portsmouth, N.H.: Heinemann, 1988.

Snow, C. E. 'Literacy and language: Relationships during the preschool years'. *Harvard Educational Review*, 53, 1983.

Spencer, M. Meek. *Learning to Read*. Portsmouth, N.H.: Heinemann, 1986.

Spencer, M. Meek. *How Texts Teach What Readers Learn*. Bath, U.K.: Thimble Press, 1988.

Thomas, K. F. 'Early reading as a social interaction process'. *Language Arts*, 62, 5, 1985.

Thomson, J. *Understanding Teenagers' Reading: Reading Processes and the Teaching of Literature*. New York: Nichols, 1987.

Vygotsky, L. S. in M. Cole, V. Scribner, E. Souberman, eds. *Mind in Society*. Cambridge, Mass.: Harvard University Press, 1978.

Wagoner, S. A. 'Comprehension monitoring: What it is and what we know about it'. *Reading Research Quarterly*, 18, 3, 1983.

## CHILDREN'S BOOKS CITED

Armstrong, William H. *Sounder*. New York: Harper & Row, 1969.

Baker, Jeannie. *Where the Forest Meets the Sea*. New York: Greenwillow, 1988.

Blume, Judy. *Forever*. New York: Bradbury Press, 1975.

Blyton, Enid. *The Enchanted Wood*. London: Darrell Waters Ltd, 1939.

Boorman, John. *Hope and Glory*. Winchester, Mass.: Faber & Faber, 1987.

Briggs, Raymond. *The Tin-Pot Foreign General and the Old Iron Woman*. Boston: Little, Brown & Co., 1985.

Brown, Jeff. *Flat Stanley*. New York: Scholastic, 1972.

Burningham, John. *Mr Gumpy's Outing*. New York: Penguin, 1984.

Burningham, John. *Granpa*. New York: Harper & Row Junior Books, 1967..

Burningham, John. *Where's Julius?* New York: Crown, 1987.

Byars, Betsy. *The Pinballs*. New York: Harper & Row Junior Books, 1977.

Byars, Betsy. *The Eighteenth Emergency*. New York: Viking, 1973.

Carle, Eric. *The Very Hungry Caterpillar*. New York: Putnam, 1981.

Cleary, Beverly. *Dear Mr Henshaw*. New York: Dell, 1983.

Dahl, Roald. *Fantastic Mr Fox*. New York: Penguin, 1988.

Dahl, Roald. *Boy*. New York: Penguin, 1988.

Davidson, Margaret. *Louis Braille*. New York: Scholastic, 1971.

Davidson, Margaret. *Helen Keller's Teacher*. New York: Scholastic, 1972.

Eastman, Philip D. *Are You My Mother?* New York: Random House, 1960.

Fox, Mem. *Wilfrid Gordon McDonald Partrige*. New York: Kane/Miller, 1985.

Garner, Alan. The *Stone Book Quartet*. New York: Dell, 1988.

Giff, Patricia Reilly. *Today Was a Terrible Day*. New York: Penguin, 1980.

Haak, D. *Alexander and the Terrible, Horrible, No Good, Very Bad Day*. (Based on Judith Viorst's book of the same title.) Van Nuys, Cal.: Aims Media, Inc.

Heide, Florence P. *The Shrinking of Treehorn*. New York: Dell, 1979.

Hutchins, Pat. *Don't Forget the Bacon!* New York: Greenwillow, 1976.

Hutchinson, Veronica S. 'Three billy goats gruff' in Belle Sideman, ed. *The World's Best Fairy Stories*. New York: Random House, 1967.

Jacobs, Joseph. 'The three little pigs' in Belle Sideman, ed. *The World's Best Fairy Stories*. New York: Random House, 1967.

Klein, Robin. *Penny Pollard's Diary*. New York: Oxford University Press, 1987.

L'Engle, M. *A Wrinkle in Time*. New York: Dell, 1973.

Martin, Ann M. *The Baby-Sitters Club*. New York: Scholastic, 1986.

Munsch, Robert N. *The Paper Bag Princess.* Toronto: Annick Press Ltd, 1980.

Park, Ruth. *Playing Beatie Bow.* New York: Penguin, 1984.

Paterson, Katherine. *Bridge to Terabithia.* New York: Harper & Row Junior Books, 1987a.

Paterson, Katherine. *The Great Gilly Hopkins.* New York: Harper & Row Junior Books, 1987b.

Pearce, Philippa. *Tom's Midnight Garden.* New York: Dell, 1986.

Reece, James. *Lester and Clyde.* Gosford, Australia: Ashton Scholastic, 1976.

Sendak, M. *Where the Wild Things Are.* New York: Harper & Row Junior Books, 1988.

Summerfield, G. *Junior Voices — Book 4,* Harmondsworth, U.K.: Penguin, 1970.

Thiele, Colin. *Storm Boy.* New York: Harper & Row Junior Books, 1987.

Thiele, Colin. *Farmer Schulz's Ducks.* New York: Harper & Row Junior Books, 1988.

Tolstoy, Alexei. *Great Big Enormous Turnip.* Glenview, Ill.: Scott, Foresman & Co., 1971.

Trezise, Percy & Roughsey, Dick. *The Quinkins.* Sydney: Collins, 1978.

Vaughan, Marcia K. *Wombat Stew.* Lexington, Mass.: Silver, Burdett & Ginn, 1986.

Verne, Jules. *20,000 Leagues Under the Sea.* New York: Simon & Schuster, 1954.

Viorst, Judith. *Alexander and the Terrible, Horrible, No Good, Very Bad Day.* New York: Macmillan, 1987.

Wagner, Jenny. *Aranea.* Harmondsworth, U.K.: Penguin, 1979.

Wagner, Jenny. *John Brown, Rose, and the Midnight Cat.* Harmondsworth, U.K.: Penguin, 1977.

Westall, Robert. *The Machine-Gunners.* New York: Alfred A. Knopf, 1975.

Westall, Robert. *Fathom Five.* London: Macmillan, 1979.

Wheatley, Nadia & Rawlins, Donna. *My Place.* Blackburn, Vic.: Collins Dove, 1987.

White, E. B. *Charlotte's Web.* New York: Harper & Row Junior Books, 1952.

Wilder, L. *Little House on the Prairie.* New York: Harper & Row, 1975.

Wilhelm, Hans. *I'll Always Love You.* New York: Crown Publishers, 1985,

Woods, C. 'Magic, energy and response: Literature in the language arts program'. *Orana,* 19, 1, 1983.

# Index